done in a day

Simple Remodeling

done in a day
Simple Remodeling

STEWART WALTON

TIME®
LIFE
BOOKS

Alexandria, Virginia

TIME®
LIFE
BOOKS

TIME-LIFE BOOKS IS A DIVISION OF TIME LIFE INC.

TIME LIFE INC
PRESIDENT AND CEO: GEORGE ARTANDI
TIME-LIFE CUSTOM PUBLISHING
VICE PRESIDENT AND PUBLISHER: TERRY NEWELL
VICE PRESIDENT OF SALES AND MARKETING: NEIL LEVIN
DIRECTOR OF SPECIAL SALES: LIZ ZIEHL
DIRECTOR OF ACQUISITIONS: JENNIFER PEARCE
PROJECT MANAGER: JENNIE HALFANT

TIME LIFE IS A TRADEMARK OF TIME WARNER INC. U.S.A.

LIBRARY OF CONGRESS CATALOGING-IN-PUBLICATION DATA
WALTON, STEWART.
    SIMPLE REMODELING / BY STEWART WALTON.
        P. CM. -- (DONE IN A DAY)
    INCLUDES INDEX
    ISBN 0-7370-0029-5 (ALK. PAPER)
    1. DWELLINGS -- REMODELING -- AMATEURS' MANUALS. I. TITLE.
II. SERIES: WALTON, STEWART.   DONE IN A DAY
TH4816.W354 1998
643'.7--DC21   98-28746
                                               CIP

A MARSHALL EDITION. CONCEIVED, EDITED AND DESIGNED BY MARSHALL
EDITIONS LTD
THE ORANGERY, 161 NEW BOND STREET LONDON W1Y 9PA

FIRST PUBLISHED IN THE UK IN 1998 BY MARSHALL PUBLISHING LTD
COPYRIGHT © 1998 MARSHALL EDITIONS DEVELOPMENTS LTD
ALL RIGHTS RESERVED INCLUDING THE RIGHT OF REPRODUCTION IN WHOLE OR
IN PART IN ANY FORM

PROJECT EDITOR: ESTHER LABI
ASSISTANT EDITOR: MARIANNE PETROU
DESIGNER: JOANNA STAWARZ
CONSULTANT: SALLY WALTON
PHOTOGRAPHER: GRAHAM RAE
ILLUSTRATOR: KUO KANG CHEN
ART DIRECTOR: SEAN KEOGH
DTP EDITOR: LESLEY GILBERT
MANAGING EDITOR: CLARE CURRIE
EDITORIAL COORDINATOR: REBECCA CLUNES
PRODUCTION: JAMES BANN

ORIGINATED IN SINGAPORE BY MASTER IMAGE   PRINTED AND BOUND IN ITALY

CONTENTS

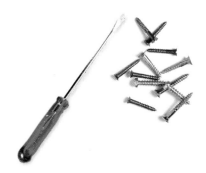

INTRODUCTION

Have you wearied of looking at the same, tired walls? Are your floors dull and boring underfoot? Perhaps the whole house needs redecorating, but you don't know where to start? The following pages show you how you can create the look you want for your home, just by investing a little time and effort.

At some time or another, you will want to redecorate your home. Whether you have the time and patience to do it all at once or just a little at a time is up to you. Within these pages you'll find twelve stunning but simple decorative ideas for every part of a room – walls, floors and ceiling – as well as for every room in the house. From adding a dignified air to a room by putting up a cornice to just revamping that old

bathroom floor, the easy-to-follow steps illustrated with detailed photography make any of the projects you attempt easy to achieve. It's up to you where you start!

Take a look around your living room – if you think your walls are a little tired and could do with a coat of paint, simple **paint effects** will certainly provide inspiration. The two paint effects shown, sponging and marbling, were chosen because a professional finish is so easily achieved. If you prefer wallpaper but can't find one you like, look at our **alternative wallpaper** to see how you can make your own. Close your eyes and imagine what your room would look like with a **chair rail and molding** added to the baseboards, then look at the steps to find out how to do it. If you are happy with the walls and it's the floor you want to concentrate on, follow our instructions and lay new **wood flooring** to a professional standard.

We haven't forgotten about any part of a room, with a **ceiling treatement** that includes putting up a cornice and a ceiling rose, and a **window dressing**, which covers putting up a roller blind as well as making a formal valance and easy, no-sew curtains. For a different look, we show you how to add **window shutters**, too!

Don't limit yourself to just one area of the house; try a whole new approach to your bathroom with a **new-look bathroom** or a just a new **bathroom floor**. You can put a little romance back into the bedroom too, with a **bed canopy** draped with billowing muslin.

Depending on how adventurous you feel, you can either follow the instructions, step by step, or adapt the project to suit your own requirements. For example, you can follow our pattern in the **mixed tile and mosaic worktop** or create your own design. You can then apply the tiling technique to any tiling situation. The **kitchen cupboard doors** are particularly flexible, with three different door options to choose from. If you want to replicate exactly what is created in the photographs, templates and diagrams are provided whenever possible. With three borders to choose from to make the alternative wallpaper and three different designs to copy for the painted kitchen cupboards, you're sure to find something you like. There are also exploded diagrams to help you see how the more complicated projects are put together.

As well as home-decorating ideas, you'll also learn simple but valuable do-it-yourself techniques that are applicable to any room and which you can use over and over again. Whether you need a complete renovation or you just want a change, remember, the twelve decorative ideas in this book can all be easily achieved – in just one day!

A NOTE ABOUT MEASUREMENTS:

The measurements and quantities given for each project are adaptable for different sizes and areas. Wherever possible, information is given to allow you to calculate how much material you will need to customize the project. When working with tiles, always allow for breakages and buy slightly more than you need. Both imperial and metric measurements are given, but only follow one set of measurements—do not interchange them.

A NOTE ABOUT WALL ANCHORS AND DRILL BITS:

Depending on the type of wall you have, you may have to use wall anchors to hold a screw in a wall. For a brick wall, use a ¼-inch (6-mm) masonry drill bit and a wall anchor; for a plaster wall, use a ⅛-inch (3-mm) drill bit and a spring-type wall anchor; for a wooden joist, use the same drill bit but no wall anchor. Wall anchors come in all shapes and sizes for different walls and weight-loads. The best way to choose the right one is to check the recommendations on the package.

Now that you are ready to attempt your first project, keep the following safety procedures in mind at all times:

❖ Several of the projects suggest protective clothing for certain steps so please wear them. Remember, accidents do happen;

❖ Always keep powertools unplugged while they are not in use;

❖ If you are working outdoors, make sure that any powertool cables are kept clear of water;

❖ When working with a scalpel or utility knife, keep your steadying hand *behind* and *well away* from your cutting hand;

❖ When drilling or screwing near cables, wires or pipes, remember to switch off the mains supply first;

❖ Only cut MDF (Medium Density Fiberboard) in a well-ventilated area and wear the correct type of breathing mask.

HOW THIS BOOK WORKS

A brief introduction describes each project

List details the equipment needed for each project

If necessary, an exploded diagram shows how elements fit together

Detailed photographs provide a visual reference to accompany the text

Boxes of information provide useful tips on products and procedures

Descriptive text accompanies each photograph, to ensure you know exactly what you are doing

Where necessary, patterns and templates are provided for you

Close-up photographs of the finished projects clearly show the end result

Some projects include a variation of the original project

'Professional Tip' boxes offer expert guidance on achieving the best results

Variations of the projects are also illustrated in detail

ALTERNATIVE WALLPAPER

If you've spent hours and hours poring over books of wallpaper samples in search of a border pattern and still can't find what you want, try this method for making your own inexpensive alternative.

TOOLS

Cutting mat

Spray adhesive

Carpenter's level

Pencil

Metal ruler

Craft knife

Tape measure

Thick sponge

Dry/Damp cloth

Paste brush

MATERIALS

❖ Border pattern, see pages 12 and 109

❖ Sheets of plain 8½-x-11-inch paper (see Step 3)

❖ P.V.A. (white) glue and old paintbrush

❖ Acrylic matte varnish and paintbrush (optional)

VARIATION

❖ Selection of old maps

❖ Wallpaper paste

❖ Tinted varnish and paintbrush

NOTES

To figure out how many copies to make of the border, measure the perimeter of the room and divide this figure by the length of the border.

For the maps, figure out the area of coverage you need by multiplying the lengths of the walls by the distance between the baseboard and chair rail. If you don't have a chair rail and want to add one, turn to Project 2 for instructions on how to put one up.

STARTING OUT - STEPS 1 TO 4

1 Choose a border from a pattern book or use the one on page 12 (the one used here) or one from page 109. Figure out the width you would like your border to be, and then photocopy the pattern, enlarging it to the correct width. Photocopy the pattern twice and then cut out both copies using a craft knife and a metal ruler on a protective cutting mat.

2 Trim the ends and check that the two pieces of the pattern will flow together. The pattern on page 12 is almost perfectly symmetrical, which means that when you place two copies of it end to end, they match almost exactly (with just a slight overlap). If you use another pattern you may have to trim it so that the pattern will match up.

3 Cover the back of the two copies with spray adhesive and press them onto a piece of 8½-x-11-inch paper. (If the border is quite large, you may need to use 11-x-17-inch paper.) Then photocopy the page as many times as you need to get the amount of coverage necessary. You do not need to use white paper; try textured or colored paper. You can also use handmade paper or color photocopies, but this can become quite expensive.

4 Cut out all the photocopies, being careful to be as neat as possible. Check that you have enough photocopies for the perimeter of the room, but allow for error and cut out a few extra.

PREPARING THE SURFACE

The best height for placing a border is about 36 inches (90cm) from the floor. But before you start pasting anything onto your walls, make sure you have enough space to work without having to stop and move furniture or bric-a-brac out of the way. Cover the floor with a drop cloth or layers of newspaper to protect it from any splashes of glue. If your walls are already covered in wallpaper you can paste the border directly onto it. If your wall is painted, remove any dirt and grime by washing down the walls.

FINISHING IT OFF - STEPS 5 TO 6

5 Pencil a straight line on the wall where the photocopied border will go. Use a carpenter's level to get the line straight. To make it easier to rule the line, tape a straight piece of wood or a long ruler to the carpenter's level with masking tape. Paste some P.V.A. glue on the back of a piece of the border and place it on the line.

6 Cover the photocopy with a piece of paper and wipe it with a cloth to smooth it out. The piece of paper will prevent the glue from getting smeared on the wall. Paste and place another section of the border next to the one on the wall, matching up the pattern and wiping it with a cloth. Continue in the same way until the border is complete. If you wish, protect your work with a coat of matte varnish.

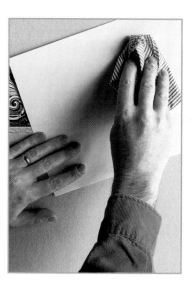

VARIATION - MAP COLLAGE

1 Once you have selected the maps you would like to use, trim off any front flaps (if they have any) leaving just the maps themselves. You will need enough maps to cover the area of wall you are working on (see Notes on page 10).

2 Atlases are another good source of material to use when designing your wallpaper (see below). Look through old atlases and pick out any pictures or colorful diagrams you would like to use. For interesting shapes for your collage, cut out round pictures, such as globes, and cut out some diagrams in wide strips.

3 Using a paste brush, spread a liberal amount of wallpaper paste evenly over the wall area. By pasting the wall as well as the back of your maps (see Step 4), you will have more flexibility in adjusting your maps to fit each other. The extra paste will also strengthen the bond between the maps and the wall. Expect half a day for the paste to dry.

4 Lay your first map face down on a paste table or work surface and apply a generous amount of wallpaper paste to its reverse side. It is easier to work on a surface large enough for the maps to sit flat. This will help you avoid handling the wet maps too much and will help keep the area as clean as possible.

CHOOSING MAPS

Inexpensive maps for the collage can be bought at garage sales or at secondhand bookstores, but bear in mind that maps and books from such places will most likely be old and out of date. School atlases, which can also be found in these places, can be a good source of diagrams to cut out (see Step 2). When looking for maps, try to find maps that include sea areas on them. The blue color of the sea breaks up the text of a map and these maps are more visually appealing than those of inland areas only.

PUTTING IT TOGETHER - STEPS 5 TO 8

5 Place the pasted map on the wall, smoothing it down temporarily with a damp cloth. Allow about an inch of the top of the map to overlap the picture rail if you have one, or ceiling. Then, in order to score the map, run the blunt edge of a pair of scissors along the crease at the edge of the wall.

6 Peel back the top part of the map to allow you to cut along the scored line. Once you have cut this strip, use the paste brush to apply a little more paste to the exposed area of the wall and smooth the entire map firmly down with a damp cloth.

7 Take the second map and apply wallpaper paste as described in Step 4. Using your fingertips, gently slide this second map along the wall so that it butts up against the edge of the map already on the wall. Smooth the second map firmly on the wall using the damp cloth.

8 As you progress, you may find that some sections of map will not stick very well. If this happens, peel back the appropriate sections and apply more wallpaper paste to the wall. Again, smooth the map down with a damp cloth.

WORKING WALLPAPER

Instead of a collage of maps on the wall, you may prefer to use one large comprehensive working map, which can be aesthetically pleasing as well as educational. This can be particularly useful in a child's room. To achieve this, you will need an up-to-date map that is large enough to cover the area between the baseboard and the chair rail. Using small-scale maps will involve careful cutting and fitting in order to match up the text correctly, so use large-scale maps if you can.

FINISHING IT OFF – STEPS 9 TO 12

9 When you have pasted up the maps, you may find that you are left with gaps along the bottom or top edge of the wall. To correct this, use some of the strips that were prepared in Step 2 to fill in any gaps. These should be pasted as before and smoothed onto the wall with a damp cloth.

10 Take a step back from your map wallpaper and decide which areas need extra shape and color. Place particularly colorful maps or some of the round cut-out shapes in these places and smooth them down as before.

11 Using a damp sponge, smooth out any air bubbles that may have appeared on the wallpaper. Wipe down the baseboard and chair rail with a sponge and warm water to remove any excess wallpaper paste.

12 Using a paintbrush, apply one coat of tinted varnish over the wallpaper. The tinted varnish slightly ages the maps and gives the overall area a softer feel. It also allows you to clean the area more easily. Do not be alarmed if the varnish appears to bubble and lift the maps away from the wall; the paper will dry back in place.

MORE ALTERNATIVES

If the use of maps as wallpaper doesn't appeal to your taste, there are various other alternatives that can be used in the same manner. Any material that is graphically interesting will be effective as a wallpaper and will add character to a room. Materials with visual appeal can include music manuscripts, comics, and foreign newspapers. Make sure the paper is in good condition before you paste it onto your wall, and once there, age it with a coat of tinted varnish.

CHAIR RAIL AND MOLDING

Sometimes it's simple things that can produce the greatest changes. Make lofty rooms more cozy or simply add a touch of elegance by adding molding to the baseboards and a chair rail to the walls. Accentuate the look with a cleverly chosen coat of paint.

TOOLS

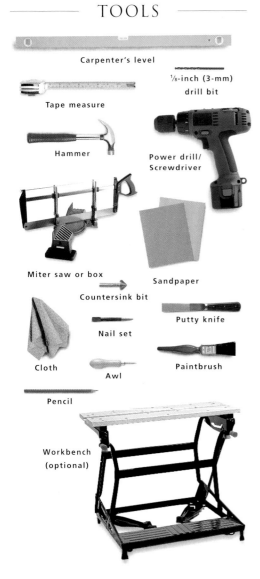

Carpenter's level

Tape measure

⅛-inch (3-mm) drill bit

Hammer

Power drill/ Screwdriver

Miter saw or box

Sandpaper

Countersink bit

Nail set

Putty knife

Cloth

Awl

Paintbrush

Pencil

Workbench (optional)

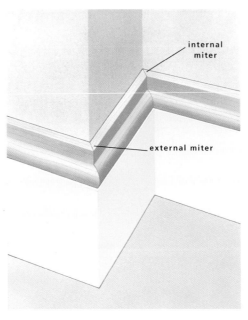

internal miter

external miter

MATERIALS

❖ Wood molding (see below)

❖ Shellac

❖ Finishing nails, ¾ inch (2cm) and 1¾ inches (4.5cm) long

❖ Wall anchors (optional, see Step 12)

❖ No. 8 wood screws, 1¾ inches (4.5cm) long

❖ Quick drying filler (wood-colored optional)

❖ Matte water-base paint

❖ Scrap piece of wood

NOTES

To figure out how much molding you need, measure the perimeter of the room, then add another 5 percent to allow for error. Most stores sell a large selection of different molding; it is usually sold in 8-foot (2.4-m) lengths.

The drill bit you need depends on the type of wall you will be drilling into (see Step 12).

STARTING OUT - STEPS 1 TO 4

1 Take a length of molding and position it firmly on the existing baseboard of the longest wall. (This will ensure that as little material as possible is wasted when cutting lengths of wood to size.) Use a pencil to mark the top edge of the molding at the point where the molding meets the corner of the wall.

2 Use a miter saw or box to miter cut the molding, ensuring the blade of the saw is lined up with the mark on the molding. Cut an internal or external miter as appropriate (see diagram on page 18 and on page 110). If your walls are uneven and the corners are not perfect right angles, you will have to cut the molding using a technique called scribing (see below).

3 Repeat Steps 1 and 2 until you have cut all the lengths of molding for the room. Position the first two pieces of molding on the baseboard to check that the mitered corners fit neatly. Hammer 1¾-inch (4.5-cm) finishing nails only halfway into the base of the molding (see Step 5). If you hammer them all the way in you will damage the molding with the hammer head. Space out the nails at roughly 16-inch (40-cm) intervals.

4 Position the next piece of molding onto the baseboard and secure it with evenly spaced finishing nails, hammered only halfway in as before. If the two pieces of molding join on an external corner, secure the joint by driving two ¾-inch (2-cm) finishing nails into either side of the molding.

SCRIBING

To scribe cut (see Step 2), first take a scrap piece of the molding to use as a marking piece. Place the scrap piece on the first length of molding so that the feature faces inward, down the length of wood you are going to use. Mark the wood to the required length by drawing around the shape of the scrap piece and cut around the shape at a 90-degree angle, using a jigsaw. The cut end of this piece of molding will now fit at right angles over the shape of a second piece of molding.

PUTTING IT TOGETHER - STEPS 5 TO 8

5 Continue fitting each length of molding until all your pieces of molding have been fitted. Now, using a hammer and a nail set go back over the nails in the molding and drive each one in fully, securing the molding to the top of the baseboard. Using a nail set will protect the molding from the head of the hammer.

6 To fit a chair rail, you need to mark out the position of the rail around the room first. Use a tape measure to measure 36 inches (90cm) up from the floor and mark this height in pencil at intervals along each wall. Use a level to join up the marks, forming a continuous line around the room.

7 Measure the length of the first wall from corner to corner and transfer the measurement onto a length of molding. Miter cut both ends of the molding as described in Step 2. To avoid wasting any material, accuracy is essential when measuring and miter-cutting lengths of wood (see below).

8 Using a ⅛-inch (3-mm) drill bit, drill pilot holes in the center section of the molding at roughly 18-inch (45-cm) intervals. The molding should be positioned on top of a scrap piece of wood to avoid any damage to your work area when drilling the wood; alternatively, use a workbench.

CUTTING MOLDING

When marking and cutting lengths of molding, it is always better to overcut and trim the piece down to size, than undercut and be left with a length of wood that is too short to use. It is also better to measure and cut molding for the longest walls first; this will leave you with smaller pieces of molding with ends that are already mitered. These can then be used to fit shorter walls and will only need to be mitered at one end. Remember, if there are any gaps at the corners, you can cover them with filler.

PUTTING IT TOGETHER - STEPS 9 TO 12

9 Now, countersink each pilot hole you have made. Apply even pressure when countersinking, but be careful not to drill too far into the wood. The countersink allows space for the screw heads on the molding and does not need to be too deep.

10 Before fixing the rail in position, apply a coat of shellac over any knots in the wood. Knots are resinous and will cause discoloration of any paint applied on top of them. Shellac acts as a sealant and will prevent discoloration.

11 Once the shellac has dried, position your rail on the wall so that the top edge of the molding is aligned with the pencil line. Use an awl to mark the wall through all the existing holes on the molding. These marks indicate the position of the holes to be made on the wall.

12 Drill holes along the length of the wall at each of the marked positions. Hold the drill straight and firmly when drilling your holes. The type of wall you are working on will determine which drill bit you use. If you are drilling into studs use a ⅛-inch (3-mm) drill bit. If your walls are brick and plaster, use a ¼-inch (6-mm) masonry drill bit and wall anchors.

WOOD QUALITY

The quality of wood is shown in the end grain. When choosing pieces of wood to work with, check the amount of curvature in the end grain of the wood. If you were to draw a circle of concentric rings to represent a cross-section of a tree trunk, then draw vertical lines over the circles to represent planks of wood, you would see that the grain on planks nearest the center is the least curved. Wood with fewer curves in the grain is better quality than wood with more pronounced curves, because these will have a tendency to bend.

FINISHING IT OFF – STEPS 13 TO 16

13 Any holes made in brick and plaster walls also require suitable wall anchors. Position these in each hole you have drilled. It should be a tight fit, so use a hammer to knock the anchor into the hole until it is flush with the wall.

14 Hold the chair rail on the wall so that it is aligned with the pencil line. Check that the holes in the chair rail are over the holes you drilled in the wall; if they aren't, the chair rail may be upside down. Then, place a no.8 screw in each hole in the molding and screw it into the wall anchor, securing the rail firmly to the wall.

15 Use a small putty knife to apply a quick-drying filler over each screw head. (If you are not going to paint the chair rail, use wood-colored filler.) You should also apply filler to any gaps between the corner joints. Once the filler has dried, rub the area down with sandpaper and wipe over the rail with a damp cloth to remove any dust.

16 Finally, paint the baseboard and the chair rail with a one-coat paint, which can be painted directly onto wood without the need of a primer. To make a feature of the chair rail, you can also paint the wall area between the chair rail and baseboard in a color a few shades darker than the rest of the room.

KEEPING YOUR MOLDING SECURE

To ensure that the chair rail and the molding are permanently positioned to the wall and baseboard, you may wish to use Liquid Nails adhesive as well as the finishing nails. Liquid Nails is a strong adhesive and forms a permanent bond with wood, so use it sparingly. It is usually supplied with an application gun and care should be taken to avoid contact with bare skin. Liquid Nails is quite viscous and should be warmed before use, but always follow the manufacturer's instructions.

WOOD FLOORING

Give an old floor a face-lift with a polished new veneer. Use wood-veneer laminated flooring panels for a professional result that belies the ease in which they are laid. For a more cost-effective change, revarnish old floorboards and add a dash of color.

TOOLS

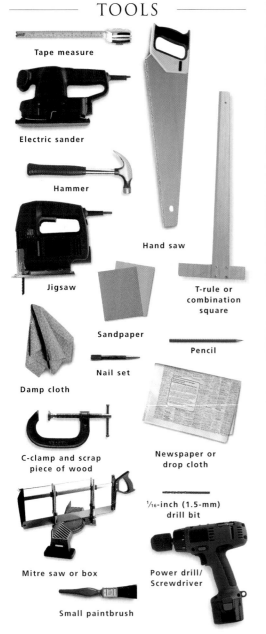

Tape measure

Electric sander

Hammer

Hand saw

Jigsaw

Sandpaper

T-rule or combination square

Pencil

Damp cloth

Nail set

Newspaper or drop cloth

C-clamp and scrap piece of wood

Mitre saw or box

¹⁄₁₆-inch (1.5-mm) drill bit

Power drill/ Screwdriver

Small paintbrush

MATERIALS

❖ Wood-veneer laminated flooring panels

❖ Quarter-round molding, see below

❖ Liquid Nails adhesive

❖ P.V.A. (white) glue

❖ Molding nails, 1½ inch (3.75cm) long

❖ Finishing nails, 1 inch (2.5cm) long

❖ No. 8 screws, 1¾ inch (4.5cm) long

❖ Piece of scrap cardboard

❖ Piece of scrap wood, to use as a buffer

❖ Wood stain in a shade to match the flooring panels

❖ Tin snips (optional), see tip box on page 27

❖ Metal scraper (optional), see Step 3

VARIATION

❖ Mineral spirits (paint thinner)

❖ Rubber gloves

❖ Tinted matte varnish

NOTE

Tongue-and-groove wood-veneer laminated flooring is usually supplied in packs. Information on the packaging will tell you how much coverage you will get per package. To figure out how much molding you will need, measure each wall to determine the perimeter of the room. Don't forget to always allow for error and buy a bit extra.

STARTING OUT – STEPS 1 TO 4

1 To prepare the floor, look for any protruding nails. Push these down into the existing floorboards with a nail set and a hammer. This will ensure that the new floor you are going to lay will sit evenly on the floor below.

2 If there are any loose or squeaky floorboards in your existing floor, secure them to the joists below with No.8 screws (see below). This should eliminate any movement in the old floor when your new floor has been laid over it.

3 Use an electric sander to smooth out any imperfections on the floorboards. If there are any bits of plaster or paint that will not lift off with the sander, use a metal scraper to remove them. You can sand the floor by hand if you wish, but you will find an electric sander easier to use and more effective over a large area.

4 Measure the length of the first wall to be fitted (see Step 8) and cut your panel to size if necessary, using a saw. (When you clamp a flooring panel to your worktop, place a scrap piece of wood between the clamp and the panel to protect the surface of the panel.) Then, with the panel firmly in place, cut away the tongue along the length of the panel with a saw.

PROFESSIONAL TIP

When driving screws into existing floorboards, be careful not to screw into any electric wires or pipes beneath the floor. Turn off the electricity supply before beginning work and make a note of the direction in which your pipes run, in order to avoid placing screws in those areas. If you are unsure what lies under the floor, drill slowly and carefully. If you do find a pipe, stop drilling, fill the hole, and screw down the floorboard somewhere else. Remember, care should be taken at all times to avoid damage or injury.

PUTTING IT TOGETHER – STEPS 5 TO 8

5 Take a piece of quarter-round molding and position it on the wooden tile, flush with the edge that has the tongue removed. Use a pencil to trace the width of the molding along the full length of the tile.

6 Position the wooden tile so that the pencil-marked edge overhangs your worktop and clamp into place. Using a ⅟₁₆-inch (1.5-mm) drill bit, drill pilot holes at about 12-inch (30-cm) intervals along the tile edge, within the pencil line. Doing this now will prevent the wood from splitting when the tile is nailed to the floor along this length in Step 9.

7 On the underside of the panel apply approximately a ⅜-inch (1-cm) width of Liquid Nails around the edge. It is not necessary to cover the entire underside of the panel with adhesive; only the edges of the panel, which will be nailed down, sit tightly on the floor below.

8 Now ease your first panel into place, making sure that the edge with the pilot holes butts the baseboard. It is always best to begin along the most difficult wall first. If, for instance, there is a chimney jog or an alcove along one wall, begin work from this wall outward. This will help you avoid cutting your panels into awkward sizes later.

GETTING A PERFECT FIT

Dry fitting (checking the fit before you glue) is the best way to ensure that there will be no unsightly gaps in the new floor. When fitting a wall with a chimney jog, for example, it is important to dry fit the panels, as the two sides of a chimney jog may vary in size. Fit one side of the chimney jog first and continue dry fitting back around the other side of it. If you are left with a gap between the panels and the baseboard on this second side, cut a piece of wood to size for a neat fit. If in doubt about any of your cuts, dry fit first.

PUTTING IT TOGETHER - STEPS 9 TO 12

9 Using a hammer, drive a molding nail into each of the pilot holes along the edge of the panel. These nails will hold the panel in place until the adhesive sets. To protect the baseboard from damage, place a piece of cardboard along the back wall when driving the nails.

10 To secure the other edge of your panel to the floor, drive molding nails into the groove of the panel, at roughly 12-inch (30cm) intervals. These nails should be driven in only part of the way with the hammer to avoid damaging the panel. Use a nail set with the hammer to drive the nails the rest of the way.

11 Laying the panels down in staggered positions ensures that the end joints do not line up and gives the floor a better bond. To do this, measure and mark the center point of the panel you have laid down. Draw a line at this point across the old floor, using a T-rule or combination square to help you. This line indicates where the next panel to be positioned should end.

12 To establish the length of the second panel to be laid, measure the distance from the pencil line marked on the floor to the wall. Transfer this measurement onto a wood panel and cut it to the required length, using a saw as before.

KEEPING YOUR FLOOR TOGETHER

Driving nails into the groove of each panel could split the wood. The part of the groove that you are nailing into is fairly thin, so it is a good idea to snip off the whole point of each nail with tin snips to prevent the wood from splitting. Liquid Nails adhesive, used under the panels, should be warmed before use. Place the tube of glue on top of a radiator, electric heater, or in a very warm place for a few minutes (always check manufacturer's instructions). This will soften the adhesive, making it more workable.

PUTTING IT TOGETHER — STEPS 13 TO 16

13 To fit the second panel, in this case around a corner, you will need to measure the corner area to be cut out of the panel. To do this, line this panel up with the panel you have already laid and mark the width of the corner. To get an accurate measurement, lift the panel slightly so that the tongue sits over the board already in position and is not included in the measurement.

14 Place the panel in position so that you can mark the length of the area to be cut. Use a T-rule or combination square to help you square up the two marks on your panel to form the correct size corner area for you to cut away from the panel.

15 Clamp your panel so that the corner area you have marked overhangs the worktop and cut out the marked out corner with a jigsaw. When you cut the wood, cut on the waste-wood side of the line and use a tear guard on the jigsaw to prevent the surface of the wood panel from chipping out (see below).

16 Place the corner panel in position and check that it fits neatly. If the fit is not quite accurate, use a piece of sandpaper to shape the edges and continue to dry fit until you are satisfied. Dry fitting is a useful method to use because it allows you to make any final adjustments before the panels are glued and nailed into position.

PROFESSIONAL TIP

When cutting any wood to specific measurements, always cut on the waste side of the wood, the side of the line that is not part of the piece you need. It is safer to overcut the measurement, rather than undercut, because you can always sand back the wood for a perfect fit. When cutting along lines, peering over the top of the jigsaw directly over the penciled marks will help you stay on the lines you have drawn. Hold the jigsaw firmly but not too stiffly, and move it through the wood with a slow and steady movement.

PUTTING IT TOGETHER - STEPS 17 TO 20

17 To lay the second panel, apply Liquid Nails to the underside of your corner panel, as in Step 7. Then, using a small brush, apply a thin layer of P.V.A. glue onto the tongue of the panel to strengthen the bonding. To make the P.V.A. easier to apply, dilute it slightly with water. This will prevent too much glue from squeezing out onto the surface of the panels.

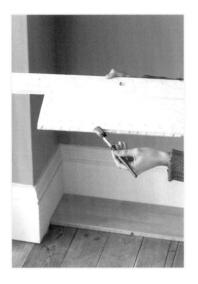

18 Position the second panel on the floor, fitting its tongue into the groove of the first panel. You will need to knock the panel into position with a hammer to ensure a tight fit. Use a scrap of wood as a buffer, to protect the panel from damage when using the hammer to knock it into place.

19 Once you are satisfied that your second panel is neatly in position, take a damp cloth and run it along the joint to clean off any P.V.A. glue that may have squeezed through onto the surface of the wooden panels.

20 Now measure and cut the third panel to the required length, and apply Liquid Nails and P.V.A. glue as before. To prevent smudging any glue over your work area, ease the panel down at an angle, placing the tongue along the width of the panel, then pushing the tongue along the length of the panel.

FITTING A SOLID FLOOR

If you decide to lay a solid wood floor, you will need to use a spacer to fit each floorboard in position. Solid wood floors expand and contract, and the use of a spacer will form a small gap between the baseboard and the floorboards to allow for the movement of the wood. Spacers can be cut out of plywood and should be positioned between the baseboard and the wood before the floorboards are secured into place. The panels used in this project are not solid wood and will not expand and contract in the same way.

FINISHING IT OFF - STEPS 21 TO 24

21 Knock the panel firmly into position with a hammer and a scrap of wood (buffer) as before. Because this panel has a tongue on both its width and length, it should be knocked in at an angle to ensure a tight fit along both of its edges. To do this, position the buffer toward the top of the panel, near the joint, and hit the corner of the buffer with the hammer.

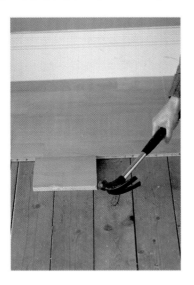

22 Continue to cut and fit each panel as before. Repeat Steps 4, 5, and 6 on all panels that butt the baseboard. When the whole floor has been covered, measure the length of one wall at a time and use a miter saw or box to miter cut your quarter-round molding to size. Cut internal or external miters as appropriate (see diagrams on pages 18 and 110).

23 Protect your work surface with sheets of newspaper or a drop cloth, and apply wood stain to the lengths of molding. The stain is applied to darken the molding to the same tone as your floor, so buy a stain that is closest in color to the floor you have chosen. Wood stain is quick-drying (check the manufacturer's instructions) and the molding can usually be positioned almost immediately after applying.

24 The molding fits along the edge of the panels and will conceal any gaps between the panels and the wall. Fix the beading to the baseboard with 1-inch (2.5-cm) finishing nails placed every 12 inches (30cm). To avoid splitting the molding, you can snip the tip off the nails first if you wish (see tip on page 27); and don't forget to use a piece of cardboard to protect your floor when you hammer them in.

LIVING WITH WOOD TILES

The panels used on this project are cost effective and easy to use. They are made with a thin layer of wood veneer, designed to look like several planks of wood joined together. The advantage of using such wood is that there are fewer joints to be made when laying the floor, giving the floor a much more seamless appearance overall. The panels are already treated and easy to clean but you should always check the manufacturer's recommendations for suitable maintenance and cleaning materials.

VARIATION - ADDING A VARNISH

1 If your floor is in good condition, color it with a tinted varnish rather than cover it with flooring panels. Prepare your floor surface by eliminating any protruding nails. Use a nail set and a hammer to drive in any nails that are sticking out above the floorboards. This will also prevent the sandpaper on your electric sander from tearing.

2 Use an electric sander to smooth over the area you wish to varnish. This should also remove any old plaster or paint that has dried on the surface. To remove stubborn bits of old plaster and paint, you may need to use a metal scraper.

3 Wipe the surface of the floor with a damp cloth to remove any residue left behind after sanding. Then, while wearing rubber gloves, wipe the floor with mineral spirits, which thoroughly clean the surface of the floor.

4 Using a large paintbrush, apply a coat of tinted matte varnish evenly over the surface of your floor. Tinted varnish is now available in a variety of unusual colors as well as in traditional wood tints. Apply two or three coats for a hardy surface. Several coats of tinted varnish will make the floor darker and darker. Use one coat of tinted varnish and then use clear varnish for subsequent coats.

LIMING

Liming is a traditional country-style paint finish and can be used to show off the grain of any wooden item (but not wood veneer panels). Prepare the surface of the floor by stripping it and sanding the surface smooth. Push a copper brush in the direction of the grain to remove the soft wood, then apply the liming wax, rubbing it well into the wood. When it has dried, apply wax furniture polish with wire wool to remove the liming wax. Buff the surface with a cotton cloth to produce a soft and lustrous sheen.

NEW-LOOK BATHROOM

Give your bathroom an invitingly simple rustic look with inexpensive wood paneling, finished off with a bright, light coat of paint. When you are done, add a new shower curtain for an elegant finishing touch.

TOOLS

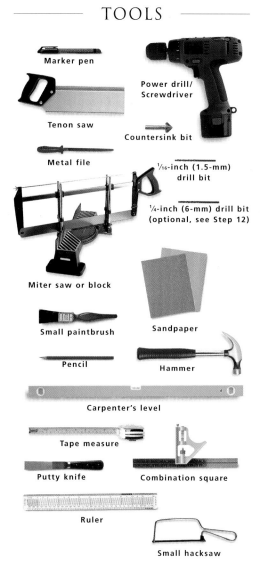

Marker pen

Power drill/Screwdriver

Tenon saw

Countersink bit

Metal file

1/16-inch (1.5-mm) drill bit

1/4-inch (6-mm) drill bit (optional, see Step 12)

Miter saw or block

Small paintbrush

Sandpaper

Pencil

Hammer

Carpenter's level

Tape measure

Putty knife

Combination square

Ruler

Small hacksaw

MATERIALS

❖ Thin, narrow tongue-and-groove panels, for the front and perimeter of the tub

❖ Nosing, enough for the perimeter of the tub plus two times the height of the panel

❖ Piece of 1 x 4 inch (2.5 x 10cm) wood, eight times the length of your tub

❖ Piece of thin plywood, about 8 x 8 inches (20 x 20cm)

❖ No. 8 screws, 1¾ inches (4.5cm) long

❖ Wood glue

❖ Woodscrews, 1 inch (2.5cm) long

❖ No. 8 brass screws, 1½ inches (3.75cm) long, with finishing washers

❖ Finishing nails, 1½ inches (3.75cm) long

❖ Piece of scrap cardboard

❖ Shellac

❖ Quick-drying acrylic filler

❖ Waterproof sealant and applicator

❖ Oil-base paint and wood primer if necessary

❖ Wall anchors (optional, see Step 12)

VARIATION

❖ Shower curtain

❖ Curtain rail, two mounting plates with screws

❖ Plastic curtain rings

❖ Ladder

❖ Wall anchors (optional)

STARTING OUT ~ STEPS 1 TO 4

1 Start by taking a level measurement from the edge of the bathtub to the floor. Holding the level straight against the bathtub edge, make a pencil mark on the floor on the inside edge of the level. Move the level along the entire length of the tub, marking the floor at regular intervals. Use a long ruler to join the marks in one continuous line.

2 Measure and draw a line ½ inch (1.25cm) in from the line you have already made on the floor. The distance between the lines accommodates the thickness of the tongue-and-groove panels. Aligning the panels with this inner line will ensure that the wood panel will sit just in from the edge of the tub and will not jut out.

3 Continue the inner line you marked on the floor up the wall. If you wish, you can use a length of the wooden batten that fits underneath the bath. Position the batten so that its inside edge aligns with the line on the floor and butt it up against a spirit level to ensure that it is straight. Draw a pencil line along the inside edge of the batten to meet the rim of the bath. Repeat on the wall at the other end.

4 Now measure the length of the bathtub by measuring along one of the pencil lines you marked on the floor (to make sure the tape measure is straight). Deduct ¼ inch (6mm) from this measurement and cut two wooden battens to this length. (They must be slightly shorter than the tub in order to fit underneath it.) You now have two horizontal battens for the frame (called the ladder rack) for the bathtub panel.

CONCEALING NAILS

If you prefer to varnish the panels rather than paint them, you will need to hide the nails in the sides of the panels. Instead of driving the nails into the front of the panels, the nails go in at an angle, into the corner of the wood. Avoid nailing into the tongue of the panel because this will split the wood. When preparing the access panel, screw the battens onto the panel from the back, making sure that the screws are the correct length to keep them from coming through the front of the panel (see Steps 15 and 16).

PUTTING IT TOGETHER ~ STEPS 5 TO 8

5 Place the two horizontal battens side by side on a flat surface. Using a combination square and pencil, mark straight lines across both battens at 16-inch (40-cm) intervals. These pencil marks indicate the positions of the upright battens. The lines you have marked should align with the center of the uprights when they are fitted.

6 To measure the length of the uprights, place both horizontal battens, one on top of the other, on the floor next to the tub. Stand an upright batten on them and mark where it meets the bottom edge of the bathtub rim. Deduct ⅛ inch (3mm) to allow for movement when the tub is full. Cut as many uprights as you need (this will depend on the length of your bathtub).

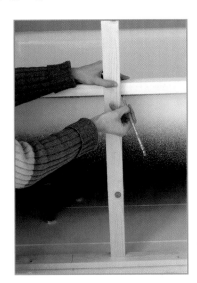

7 Use a ¼ inch (6mm) drill bit to drill and countersink two holes on each line marked on the horizontal battens. Use the No.8 screws to attach the uprights to the batten, starting in the middle of the batten followed by the ends, then add the rest of the uprights (see below).

8 Attach the other end of each upright to the other horizontal batten. This time, join the two end battens first to support the frame while you work. Make sure the battens are centered with your original marks and drive in the screws to complete the frame, or ladder rack. Then, ease the ladder rack into place, lining it up with the lines marked on the floor and on each side wall.

PROFESSIONAL TIP

In order to work easily and efficiently, it is important to allow yourself enough room in which to move around. When joining the pieces of the ladder rack (frame) together, make sure you have a flat surface, preferably an uncarpeted floor, on which to balance the rack. When attaching the upright battens to the horizontal battens, it is important that the rack does not move and that the battens are perfectly centered to avoid splitting the wood.

PUTTING IT TOGETHER - STEPS 9 TO 12

9 Using a saw, cut out small squares of thin plywood to the same size as the width of the vertical batten. Position these squares at each end of the rack, between the wall and the first vertical batten. Once you have packed in enough pieces to ensure a tight fit, screw the rack into place. Use two No.8 screws to attach the vertical battens to the wall (see below) and one screw in each bay to fix the horizontal batten to the floor.

10 In marking the end line for the frieze panel, you need to allow for the width of the nosing that will frame the frieze (see Step 21). Hold a length of nosing on the edge of the bathtub, but not so that it overhangs. Butt the outside edge of the nosing against a carpenter's level to ensure it is straight and draw a line on the wall, 18 inches (45cm) high, on the inside edge of the nosing.

11 To mark out the position of the horizontal battens for the wall frieze panel, measure and mark 18 inches (45cm) up from the tub at intervals all along the walls. Join the marks using a carpenter's level. This line marks the top of the frieze. Then, measure the length and width of the tub and cut out two pieces of each measurement for the horizontal battens. (You need two battens for each wall you panel.)

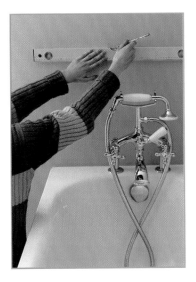

12 Lay one horizontal batten along the edge of the bathtub—the top batten is positioned so that its top edge aligns with the pencil line. Fix the top and lower battens into place using a No.8 screw placed every 12 inches (30cm). Place vertical battens between the horizontal battens every 16 inches (40cm). Fix them to the wall with two evenly spaced out screws in each piece (see box below).

WALL ATTACHMENT

The way in which you secure the wooden battens to the wall will depend on the type of wall you are attaching them to. If you are working on a stud wall, you will need to locate the studs and screw the battens directly to them, without drilling holes into the wall. If the wall you are working on is a brick or plaster wall, you will need to drill pilot holes into the wall first, and then place a suitable wall anchor into each hole before screwing the battens into position.

PUTTING IT TOGETHER – STEPS 13 TO 16

13 The access panel is the only removable part of the bathtub panel and will allow access for plumbing. To make it, cut two pieces of tongue-and-groove to the length between the edge of the tub and the floor (see Step 1), and subtract ⅛ inch (3mm) to allow for movement when the tub is full. Apply wood glue into the groove of one piece, then press the tongue of the other board firmly into the groove.

14 On the back of the access panel, measure and draw a line 2 inches (5cm) in from the top and bottom, and 1 inch (2.5cm) in from the long sides. Cut two 6-inch (15-cm) pieces of batten and use wood glue to stick them across the panel at each short end and within the pencil marks.

15 Now turn the panel over. You need to reinforce the glued batten with screws. Mark the location of the battens by drawing the same outline as you did in Step 14. Using a ⅛-inch (3-mm) drill bit, drill a pilot hole through the panel into the batten underneath, at each end of the batten.

16 To complete the access panel, countersink the pilot holes you have made, keeping the countersink fairly shallow. Screw in 1-inch (2.5-cm) woodscrews through the pilot holes to secure the battens to the access panel.

PROFESSIONAL TIP

When joining two pieces of wood together, the length of the screw you use will depend on the thickness of the top piece of wood; the screw should be long enough to go halfway through the other piece of wood. Using an awl to break the surface of the wood is a good habit to get into. The pointed end of the drill bit will rest in the awl mark and this reduces the likelihood of the drill slipping. Always use the correct screwdriver for the screw. If the blade is too wide it will slip out; too narrow and it will chew up the slot.

PUTTING IT TOGETHER - STEPS 17 TO 20

17
Position the access panel so that the tongue of the panel is next to the wall. Drill a pilot hole in the center top and center bottom of each panel, using a ⅛-inch (3-mm) drill bit. Drill through the access panel and into the horizontal batten around the bath to a depth of 1 inch (2.5cm). Attach the access panel with a hand screwdriver and the brass screws with finishing washers.

18
Cut the number of tongue-and-groove panels needed to complete the bathtub panel to the length calculated in Step 13. When fitting a panel next to the access panel, place groove next to groove to allow for the removal of the access panel. Attach all the tongue-and-groove panels with a finishing nail in each corner. Remember to put glue on both the tongue and groove of each piece and on the horizontal battens.

19
Measure and cut the number of tongue-and-groove panels for the frieze. They should be flush with the top edge of the top horizontal batten. Starting on the back wall in a corner, fit the panels along the wall with finishing nails in the upper and lower battens. The first panel should be positioned so that the tongue is in the corner. Use a piece of scrap cardboard to protect the tub when hammering.

20
Once you have fitted all the panels along the back wall, fit the side panels in the same way, working from the corners to the outside edges. Fitting the panels in this order allows you to cut the last panel on the edge to the correct size, rather than the corner panel. Cut the end panel to size so that it sits flush with the edge of the end batten. Remember to remove the tongue to achieve a straight edge.

DEALING WITH AWKWARD SPACES

When fitting the frieze panels into position, you may have difficulty accessing the area behind the faucets. It is not a good idea to attempt to drive any finishing nails into the base of the panels with a hammer, because you could damage your taps. It is best to either remove the faucets altogether to allow you to work freely, or use a nail set with the hammer to hit the nails into position without damaging the faucets. When hammering close to the bathtub or floor, always use a piece of scrap cardboard to protect the surface.

FINISHING IT OFF – STEPS 21 TO 24

21 Measure and cut a piece of nosing the length of the back panel, mitering any corners. Be as accurate as possible to ensure a neat fit. Place wood glue along the top of the back panel and position the nosing with the rounded edge facing outward, over the bathtub. Nail the nosing to the batten with finishing nails spaced at 12-inch (30-cm) intervals. Use a piece of cardboard to protect the wall against damage from the hammer.

22 Measure and cut the nosing for the side: cut it slightly longer than necessary so that you can miter the end to fit the corner. To do this, draw a straight line on the nosing, level with the end of the side panel. With your pencil at the bottom of the line you have just drawn, draw a diagonal line outward, to indicate the direction of the end miter cut.

23 Now take another piece of nosing and stand it vertically against the end of the side panel. Mark a straight line on the nosing, level with the top edge of the panel. Then draw a miter line from this mark upward, across the depth of the nosing. Cut both pieces of nosing and miter-cut both pieces to fit each other. Glue and nail the lengths of nosing into place as before.

24 Apply a coat of shellac over any knots in the wood to prevent discoloration when the panels are painted. Cover all the nail heads with filler and allow it to dry before sanding. Where the frieze panel meets the tub, apply a waterproof sealant to make the area watertight. When all the materials are dry, paint the panels with a coat of wood primer followed by an oil-base paint.

USING A SEALANT

A waterproof sealant prevents water from seeping in between the walls and the bathtub, wetting the walls as well the wood paneling. Regular wetting of this area could result in a problem with mold on the walls or the wood rotting. When applying the sealant, work slowly, making sure it fills the gap. Some sealants take 24 hours to dry, so leave enough time before using the tub. Make sure the sealant you purchase is mold resistant and flexible; a bathtub moves slightly when it is full.

VARIATION – ADDING A SHOWER RAIL

1 Unfold and lay the shower curtain out on a work surface, ensuring you have enough space for the full curtain to lie flat. Use a tape measure to measure the drop. This measurement will allow you to figure out the height of the curtain pole (see Step 5).

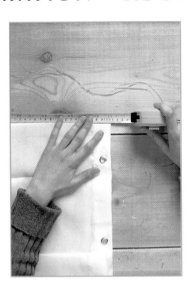

2 Using a tape measure, measure the length of the bathtub to determine the length of pole needed. This will only be an accurate measurement if the tub sits in an alcove. If the distance between the two walls is more than the length of the bathtub, you will need to cut the pole accordingly. Transfer the required measurement to the pole, using a marker pen.

3 Position the pole on a piece of scrap wood with the marked section overhanging the edge of your work surface. Hold the pole firmly in position and use a small hacksaw to cut it to the required length.

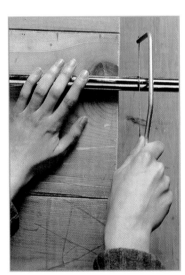

4 Once you have cut the pole, you will be left with a sharp edge that will need filing down. Use a metal file to smooth down the sharp edges.

CUTTING PIPES

Hacksaws are specially designed for cutting metal or plastic pipes and are available in two sizes. The smaller sized is suitable for most jobs around the house. Hacksaw blades are changeable, and you normally need a separate blade for cutting steel. However, if you intend to cut a lot of tubing or have a large plumbing job that involves cutting pipes, you may want to consider getting a pipe cutter, which is quicker and more accurate than a hacksaw and is adjustable for different-sized pipes.

PUTTING IT TOGETHER – STEPS 5 TO 8

5 Take the curtain measurement from Step 1 and subtract 8 inches (20cm). Transfer this measurement onto each side wall, measuring from the top of the tub upward with a tape measure. This mark indicates the height at which your curtain pole should be attached, allowing 8 inches (20cm) of the curtain to drop inside the bathtub.

6 Now use a tape measure to measure the width of your bathtub. Butt the end of the tape measure against the back wall and measure to the outside edge of the bathtub. This measurement will help ensure that the curtain pole is placed at the correct distance from the back wall.

7 Use a tape measure to transfer the measurement taken in Step 6 onto each side wall. The point where the height mark meets the width mark represents the position at which the curtain pole should be fixed above the bathtub.

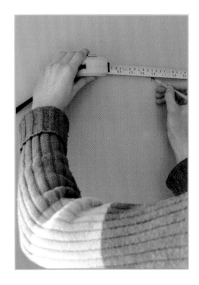

8 Position a mounting plate on one of the side walls, making sure it is centered on the mark you have made. The mounting plate will either come with screws or specify the size of screw you need. If you are working on brick or plaster walls you will need to drill holes into the wall and fit suitable wall anchors into the holes (see below) before screwing the mounting plate into position.

WALL ANCHORS

A visit to your local hardware store will surprise you with the variety of wall anchors available. Wall anchors can be divided roughly into two groups: those for solid walls and those for hollow walls, ceilings, and lightweight blocks. Some are metal with spring toggles, others are plastic, and others are plastic with wings! To choose the right wall anchor, first determine what kind of wall you have. Then, read the back of the package; it will usually explain what kind of wall the anchors are suitable for and what kind of weight they can take.

FINISHING IT OFF – STEPS 9 TO 12

9 One end of the curtain pole can now be placed into the mounting plate on the wall. Slide the pole into the center of the plate, keeping it as straight as possible. Balance the other end of the pole on a ladder in order to keep it straight and to prevent it from coming out of the wall plate.

10 Before attaching the other mounting plate, check that the pole will be straight when the end sits on the height mark you have made. Use a carpenter's level and adjust the height mark on the wall if necessary. Checking this now, before the second plate is fixed, may save you refitting the wall plates later.

11 To attach the other end of the pole to the wall, first slide the mounting plate onto the pole and straighten the pole so that the end is flat on the wall. Then slide the mounting plate back along the pole until it sits flat on the wall and attach it to the wall as described in Step 8.

12 Loop the plastic curtain rings over the pole, then place one ring through each curtain hole, clicking the rings into position to secure the curtain to the pole.

SHOWER CURTAINS

Research the types of shower curtains available in your area before you buy one, because all shower curtains are not the same. The quality of curtain can vary quite dramatically, and this is usually reflected in the price. The thickness of the shower curtain is a good indication of quality; light, thin curtains tend to flap around in the shower while heavier curtains hang better. Many of the heavy-weight curtains can also be washed in the washing machine, which is a factor you may want to consider.

KITCHEN CUPBOARD DOORS

If your kitchen cabinets look outdated but are still in good condition, why not give your kitchen a whole new look simply by revamping the doors? With three styles here to choose from, you're sure to find one that appeals to you.

TOOLS

Jigsaw

Scissors

Sable paintbrushes Nos. 1, 4

Hammer

Tin snips

Sandpaper

Large/medium paintbrush

Pencil

Tape measure or ruler

Small dish to use as a palette

Fine steel wool

Miter saw or box

Staple gun

Tenon saw

Power drill/ Screwdriver

C-clamp

¹³⁄₆₄-inch (5-mm) drill bit

MATERIALS

For one painted door:

❖ Transfer paper

❖ Masking tape

❖ Water-base paint in green, lemon yellow, red, and ivory

❖ P.V.A. (white) glue

❖ Acrylic matte varnish

For one screen door:

❖ Steel mesh insect screen (see below)

❖ Screen molding

❖ Finishing nails, 1 inch (2.5cm) long

❖ Water-base paint, the same color as the existing doors

For one tongue-and-groove paneled door:

❖ Tongue-and-groove panels (see below)

❖ Finishing nails, 1 inch (2.5cm) long

❖ Decorative door knobs or handles

❖ Water-base or oil-base paint (optional)

NOTE

Before you start, figure out how much material you will need. This will depend on the size of your doors and number of doors you are going to change. Take careful measurements, but always allow for error and buy a little extra.

STARTING OUT ~ STEPS 1 TO 4

1 Remove the doors you are going to work on. If the door is unvarnished wood, the paint will be easily absorbed. If the door is varnished or made of any other material, sand it down with sandpaper first to provide a good base for the paint. Then paint the front of the first door with a coat of green water-base paint and leave it to dry.

2 Photocopy one of the motifs on pages 106, 107 and 108; you may have to enlarge it to fit the panel. Place a sheet of transfer paper underneath the photocopy and stick the two pieces to the door with masking tape. Make sure that the chalky side of the transfer paper is face down on the door.

3 Trace around the pattern with a sharp pencil, keeping the two sheets of paper firmly in position with one hand. The transfer paper will transfer the pattern onto the door. An alternative method is to shade in the back of your photocopy with a soft pencil and transfer the pattern by tracing over it using a pen or hard pencil.

4 Dilute the lemon yellow water-base paint using one part water to two parts paint. Then, with the No.4 sable paintbrush, paint the floral motifs, stems, and basket. Steady the hand you are painting with by allowing your wrist to rest lightly on your free hand.

COLORS AND PATTERNS

The colors used in this project are merely suggestions. Any colors can be used and you should try to match the colors with the existing color-scheme in your kitchen. The motifs provided on pages 106, 107, and 108 are also only suggestions and you should feel free to find inspiration from other sources. There are numerous pattern books available in which you may find an appropriate motif for a particular theme or period. Or you could, of course, design your own motif and trace it in the same way.

PUTTING IT TOGETHER – STEPS 5 TO 8

5 Rinse your paintbrush in water and use red paint to fill in the leaf motifs on the pattern. Apply the paint in gentle, swift strokes, being careful not to use too much pressure on the brush. To make more of a feature of the floral motifs, add a few touches of red to the areas in lemon yellow.

6 Use a finer, No.1 sable brush to apply a thin line of ivory colored paint around all the motifs. Outlining the pattern in this way gives the design unity. Use the paint liberally and be confident with your brush strokes.

7 If you have a border area around the door panel, you can block it in with a coat of ivory water-base paint. Add water to thin the paint so that it dries quickly, then apply it fairly crudely with a wide paintbrush. Once the paint has dried, rub down the entire surface of the door with a piece of fine steel wool. This will give it an aged, almost antique, effect.

8 Thicken and lighten quick-drying varnish by adding some P.V.A. glue. Use equal parts of glue and varnish and add a little water. Apply a layer of matte varnish over the surface of the door to seal and protect the painted motif. The varnish will also make it easier to clean the door. Continue painting and varnishing any other doors in the same way.

PROFESSIONAL TIP

Folk art, by its very nature, is irregular and non-symmetrical, which is what gives it its charm. It is not essential, therefore, that you paint your motif with precision. It is perfectly acceptable to paint outside the markings and to vary the thickness of the paint. Such variations, which allow the grain of the wood to show through in certain places, are characteristic of folk art. For a bold end result, use gentle, swift brush strokes and avoid hesitation once you begin a stroke.

VARIATION - SCREEN DOORS

1 To fit the doors with a sheet of insect screen you first need to cut out a panel from each door. If they do not have an obvious panel, mark one out, leaving a border of at least 3 inches (7.5cm) around the edge. Position the first door on a worktop and clamp it with the back of the door facing upward. Drill a hole in the corners of the marked-out panel, so that you can insert the blade of the jigsaw; then cut out the panel.

2 Trace a line on the back of the door around the cut-out opening, using a piece of the screen molding as a guide. The molding will eventually be positioned so that it fits flush with the edge of the insect screen on the back of the door to create a neat finish.

3 Place a piece of insect screen over the door and use a pair of tin snips to cut it to fit within the guidelines drawn in Step 2. Place the screen on the back of the door and staple it first in two opposite corners. Then, pull the screen taut, and staple the other two corners. Continue stapling the sides while pulling the screen taut until it is secure on all four sides.

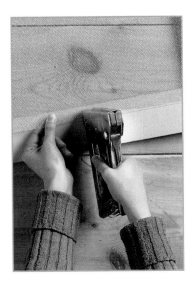

4 Cut the four lengths of screen molding, mitering the corners so that they fit neatly around the cut-out panel. Snip the ends off the finishing nails and drive them into the molding, to secure it in position. For a neat finish, paint the molding with water-base paint. Fit screens to your other doors in the same way.

PROFESSIONAL TIP

When cutting the panels, do not cut too closely to the frame of the door. As you run the jigsaw around the panel, make sure you keep the blade away from the edges of the frame to prevent the blade from cutting into them. If you leave a space between the blade and the frame, you can sand away the extra wood with sandpaper later. Another good idea is to cover the shoe plate of the jigsaw with masking tape to avoid scratching the paintwork on the doors.

VARIATION – TONGUE-AND-GROOVE PANELING

1 Cut two 1-inch (2.5-cm) strips, the same width as the door, from a plank of tongue-and-groove. Slightly bevel their edges by sanding them. Place the strips across the top and bottom of the door and attach them to the door with finishing nails placed at regular intervals. To prevent the wood from splitting, you can snip the ends off the finishing nails first.

2 Measure the distance between the inside edges of the two strips. Cut the first panel of tongue-and-groove to this length. You need to place the first panel in the exact center of the door. To do this, measure and mark the midpoint of the panel, and mark the midpoints of the strips on the door. Then line up the marks. Making sure that the first piece is centered in this way will give the door a more solid appearance.

3 To establish the width of the two end strips, fit the tongue-and-groove from the center panel back to the edges of the door without nailing them in place. Cut the number of pieces you need to the correct length and put them in place, fitting tongue into groove as you go along. Now measure and cut the end strips to size (they should be equal) and bevel the ends. Attach one of the end strips to the door as described in Step 1.

4 Remove the panels of tongue-and-groove from the door, with the one end strip in place. Then refit the pieces one by one, fitting the tongue of one into the groove of another. Tap two finishing nails into the tongue of each piece, one at each end, to secure it firmly in position. Complete the door by attaching the second end strip to the door. You can now panel your other doors in the same way.

FINISHING TOUCHES

Once you have fitted all your units with tongue-and-groove panels, the doors can be decorated according to taste. If you are painting your doors, cover any visible finishing nails with filler and sand back when dry. The doors can be painted with a one-coat paint, which cuts out the use of primer, or it can be stained in a traditional color or a more unusual shade. All woodstains allow the grain of the wood to show through. The cupboard doors can be embellished with decorative hinges or unusual knobs.

MIXED TILE AND MOSAIC COUNTERTOP

Add a burst of color to your kitchen with these "mix and match" tiles. Create your own design to match the existing color scheme of your kitchen or go for a completely new look with this practical and fun way to improve a countertop.

TOOLS

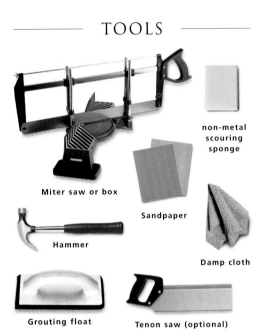

Miter saw or box

non-metal scouring sponge

Sandpaper

Hammer

Damp cloth

Grouting float

Tenon saw (optional)

Tiling trowel

Thick sponge

Tile cutter

Putty knife

Utility knife

Tape measure

Pencil

Carpenter's level

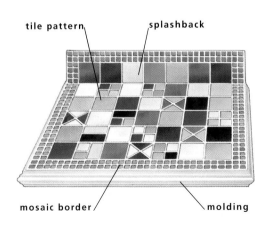

tile pattern   splashback

mosaic border   molding

MATERIALS

❖ Ceramic tiles (see below) including mosaic tiles for border

❖ Wood molding (see below)

❖ Finishing nails (see below)

❖ All-purpose ceramic tile adhesive and grout and applicator

❖ Sheet of paper

❖ Colored pencils or markers

❖ Quick-drying filler

❖ Small can of water-base paint in a color to match your existing decor

❖ Plywood for spacers

❖ Thin stick or dowel, sanded to make a rounded end

❖ Ready-made tile spacers (optional)

NOTES

To work out the size of the area you need to tile, multiply the length by the width of the worktop. Then do the same for the area of the splashback and add the two figures together. Don't forget to buy a few extra tiles to allow for breakages and error.

The molding has to fit around the perimeter of your worktop, so measure each side of the worktop, and then add the figures together. The finishing nails need to be long enough to go through the molding you choose and ¾ inch (2cm) into the worktop.

If you tile around a sink, make sure you apply silicone sealant where the sink and tiles meet.

STARTING OUT – STEPS 1 TO 4

1 With a sharp utility knife, score diagonal lines across the surface of the area you want to tile at approximately 1-inch (2.5-cm) intervals. Score from left to right, then change direction to score from right to left, forming a crisscross pattern. This is known as crosshatching and must be done to provide a good base for anchoring the tiles.

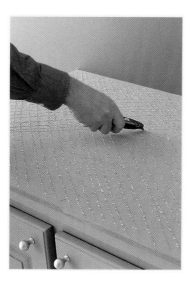

2 Measure and miter lengths of wooden molding to fit around the edges of the countertop. Place two of the thickest tiles on top of each other against the edge of the countertop and temporarily nail on the strips of molding to the same level as the tiles. The height of two tiles is about the same as the height of a tile plus adhesive; and the molding will give you an edge to work to when tiling.

3 Take one whole tile and two rows of mosaic tiles (see Step 4) and place them against the back wall. Use a pencil to mark their combined height, remembering to allow for a grouting space between them. Mark the same height at intervals along the back wall, then draw a straight line with a pencil and a level to indicate the top of the tiled area of the splashback. Crosshatch within the marked-out area (see Step 1).

4 Two-row lengths of mosaic tiles will be used to form a border around the tiled countertop and splashback. Use a tape measure to measure the length of border needed and, using a sharp utility knife, cut the required number of strips from the mosaic sheets. (It is not necessary to use a cutting mat, as any surface damage will eventually be tiled over.)

CHOOSING TILES

When choosing tiles, ask your supplier whether the tiles are sufficiently heat resistant to use on a kitchen countertop that will be exposed to hot cookware. As well as being heat resistant, they should provide be practical too, so check for stain resistance. When choosing your tiles, be as creative as you like, but try to chose tiles of the same thickness. This will make it easier when it is time to lay them, since tiles that differ in thickness will pose problems when you are trying to make the surface level (see Step 12).

PUTTING IT TOGETHER - STEPS 5 TO 8

5 Use a tile cutter to cut any ceramic tiles you wish to form patterns with. (It is helpful to have a rough idea of your design before cutting the tiles.) A tile cutter can cut any straight line and can therefore be used to make triangles, rectangles, and smaller squares. To cut a tile, use the cutter to score the enamel on the surface of the tile. The tile can then be held in both hands and snapped in half (see below).

6 With your tiles cut to the required shapes and sizes, you can now begin to build up your final design. You can copy the pattern used here (see diagram on page 54) or create your own. Experiment with designs by placing the tiles, without adhesive, on the entire countertop area, leaving gaps for the grouting.

7 When you are satisfied with the design, use colored pencils to sketch a record of it. Alternatively, if you have a Polaroid camera, you can photograph it. When you have recorded the design, lift the tiles off. It is a good idea to stack the tiles in the order in which they should be laid down; it will help when it is time to refit them.

8 Using a tiling trowel, spread a layer of all-purpose ceramic tile adhesive evenly over a section of the work surface. Work with small areas at a time; it is always useful to have a clean surface available while work is in progress.

PROFESSIONAL TIP

If you are using particularly thick tiles you may have difficulty snapping them in half, even after they have been scored with the tile cutter. If this is the case, lay a match on the table and place your tile on top of the match, aligning it with the score line of the tile. With both hands, press down on either side of the tile to snap it in half. Using a match in this way creates a tiny gap between the tile and the work surface to give you extra leverage.

PUTTING IT TOGETHER ~ STEPS 9 TO 12

9 Now use the toothed end of the tiling trowel to comb through the adhesive, working in one direction only. The teeth form trails of adhesive that are all the same height. This ensures that the tiled surface remains level and prevents any tiles from sinking.

10 In order to determine where the first tiles are going to sit, place pieces of the mosaic border at intervals along the edges temporarily, to indicate the width of the border. Begin laying down the larger tiles, positioning them as evenly as possible in each row and leaving gaps for grouting. You can judge the gaps by eye or use a spacer. Remember to leave a gap between the last tile and the splashback.

11 When you have laid the main countertop area, you can work on the border. Since the mosaic tiles are not usually as thick as larger ones, you will need to add extra grout along the border area to bring them up to the same level. If an applicator is supplied with your adhesive, cut it to the width of the border and use it to apply more adhesive. Otherwise, use a piece of thick cardboard to spread it.

12 Then lay the two-row strips of mosaic tiles down to form the border. Use a spirit level or scrap piece of wooden batten to check the level matches that of the larger tiles. If it does not, remove the mosaic tiles and add more adhesive until the tiles are level.

ADHESIVE AND GROUT

The all-purpose ceramic tile adhesive and grout used in this project is ready-to-use and dries white. This makes it easier to use than the traditional separate adhesive and grout, which differ in color. Traditional adhesive is dark in color while the grout used is white.

This means that the dark adhesive will show through the grout in dark patches. If you wish to use separate adhesive and grout, buy a dark-colored grout to disguise the color of the adhesive and to prevent dark patches from showing through.

PUTTING IT TOGETHER – STEPS 13 TO 16

13 Use a damp sponge to wipe off any lumps of adhesive that have squeezed through over the surface of the tiles. It is important to clean the tiles as you go along or the adhesive may set.

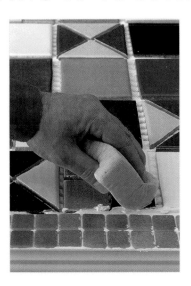

14 Use the tiling trowel to spread the adhesive and comb over the splashback area. Cut enough spacers out of plywood to sit on the tiles closest to the back wall. The spacers should be equivalent in thickness to the gaps between the tiles so you may need to cut two for each tile, depending on the thickness of your plywood.

15 Place the tiles on the back wall one by one, ensuring that each tile is sitting on a spacer. Press them firmly into position and continue until all the large tiles forming the splashback are fitted. Then build up the adhesive and add the mosaic tiles as before, in Step 12.

16 Use a plastic spatula to scrape off any excess adhesive that has squeezed through onto the back wall as well as any lumps on the surface of the tiles. Then wipe them down with a warm, damp sponge. However, if there is too much movement in the tiles at this stage, let the surface dry a little longer.

PROFESSIONAL TIP

If you have applied too much adhesive when tiling, do not be alarmed. The adhesive does not dry immediately so there is enough time to scrape it off and use a damp sponge to clean the area. Always try to be as neat as possible when tiling and work within the lines you have marked out. When wiping over the surface of the tiles, use as much water as you feel necessary because the area will dry and become waterproof.

PUTTING IT TOGETHER – STEPS 17 TO 20

17 Remove the molding around the edge of the worktop. Pull out the temporary nails and gently ease the molding away from the edges of the worktop.

18 Reposition the molding on the edge of the countertop so that it sits level with the tiled surface. Tap it into place with finishing nails placed at 12-inch (30-cm) intervals.

19 Wait until the adhesive is set (check the manufacturer's instructions), then apply the gout with a grouting float. Tilt the float at an angle and push a liberal amount of grout into the gaps between the tiles both on the countertop and splashback.

20 Now use the grouting float to run over the entire countertop and splashback. It is safe to use the grouting float for this purpose since it has a rubber base and will not damage the surface of your tiles.

SUCCESSFUL GROUTING

It is important that you use a grouting float to apply grout to a tiled area; it will help ensure that sufficient grout is pushed into the gaps between the tiles. If the grout is *not* worked fully into the gaps, pockets of air will be left in the grout and these will surface later when it dries, forming unsightly holes. If this happens, you will then have to repeat the grouting process in order to fill in the holes and give your tiled surface a neat, professional-looking finish.

FINISHING IT OFF - STEPS 21 TO 24

21 Round off the end of a stick or a piece of thin doweling with some sandpaper. Run the tip along the adhesive at the top of the splashback to give a neat edge to the tiles. This process is known as pointing.

22 Now use a non-metal scouring sponge and warm water to clean the entire surface of the countertop. Any excess adhesive that has dried on the surface of the tiles can be easily removed with the scourer. It is important that the scourer you use does not scratch the enamel. Check its effect on a spare tile if you are not sure. This is a good time to fill any pits or bubbles between the tiles.

23 If any adhesive is sitting on the tile edges, use a bit of plywood to scrape it off and neaten the edges. This will ensure straight lines around all the tile edges and give the entire surface a neat finish.

24 Finally, use a soft dry cloth to polish the tiles to give your countertop a clean, shiny finish. Cover the finishing-nail heads in the molding with filler, and sand them when the filler has dried. Then paint the molding the same color as your cabinets to give a coordinated look to your new tiled countertop.

CARING FOR YOUR COUNTERTOP

Remember that tiles, in particular ceramic tiles, are extremely durable, but their surface can be easily scratched. Avoid placing any sharp or rough-bottomed objects on the tiled surface that may scratch it. Wipe your tiled countertop clean with a damp cloth, but do not regularly flood the area with water. If, despite your best efforts to keep the countertop looking neat and clean, the grouting does eventually discolor, rewhiten the grout with a commercially prepared grout-whitener or a weak dilution of bleach.

BED CANOPY

Introduce a note of exotic romance to your bedroom with a sumptuous bed canopy.
Sleeping beneath a veil of luxurious lengths of billowing muslin, you are sure to have
the pleasantest of dreams.

TOOLS

Jigsaw

Countersink bit

Pencil

Power drill/
Screwdriver

⅛-inch (3-mm)
drill bit

Newspaper or drop cloth

Sandpaper

Carpenter's level

Paintbrush

Ruler

Staple gun

Tape measure

C-clamp

Scissors

Workbench

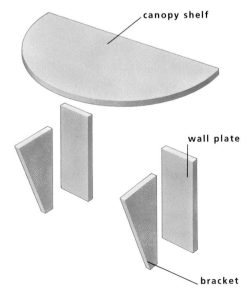

canopy shelf

wall plate

bracket

MATERIALS

❖ Piece of ¾-inch (2-cm) medium-density fiberboard (MDF), 16 x 18 inches (40 x 45cm); for alternatives, see box on page 63

❖ Wood glue

❖ No. 8 screws, 1¾ inches (4.5cm) long

❖ Small can of water-base paint the same color or complementary to your wall

❖ Muslin, 20 feet (6m) of fabric for a 6-foot (1.8-m) drop

❖ Thumbtack or small object (see Step 10)

❖ Staples for staple gun

❖ Piece of string 12 inches (30cm) long

❖ Small nail

❖ Plumbline, or string with a key tied to the end

❖ Wall anchors (optional)

STARTING OUT - STEPS 1 TO 4

1 On the piece of MDF, mark out a semicircle for the shelf. To do this, first measure and mark the midpoint of one of the 18-inch (45-cm) sides. Attach a piece of string to the midpoint with a small nail. Loop the other end of the string around a pencil and tie a knot, making the string 9 inches (22.5cm). Pull the pencil toward one corner so that the string is taut and, keeping it taut, draw a semicircle from one corner of the board to the other.

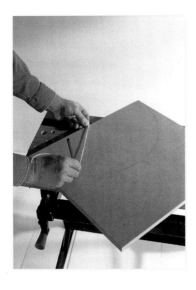

2 Now mark out two wall plates and two brackets. Draw a line 6 inches (15cm) in from the other 18-inch (45-cm) side and divide this into two rectangles, 8¾ inches (22cm) and 9¼ inches (23cm) in length. Divide one rectangle into two 9¼- x 3-inch (23- x 7.5-cm) wall plates. Divide the other of these rectangles lengthways into two brackets by drawing a diagonal line 1 inch (2.5cm) in from each of the opposite corners.

3 Secure the board to your workbench using a C-clamp. Using a jigsaw, carefully cut out all the marked pieces. When sawing, remember always to cut on the waste side of the wood; you can then sand the extra wood away.

4 To mark the position of each component, mark 3½ inches (9cm) in from each corner of the semicircle. Stand each wall plate vertically on the straight edge of the semicircle, center it on the mark you have just made, and trace around its base. Center the long side of each bracket on the edge of the penciled outline of the wall plate and trace around it to form a T-shape. Now center each bracket on a wall plate and draw around it.

MDF ALTERNATIVES

Other material can be used as an alternative to MDF to make the canopy shelf and supports for this project. Plywood, hardboard (Masonite), and chipboard are all suitable alternatives that are readily available. It is important, however, to use a tear guard on the jigsaw when cutting these materials, to prevent them from splintering. Whichever material you choose to use, if you are not confident about working with wood, have it cut to size for you at your lumberyard.

PUTTING IT TOGETHER – STEPS 5 TO 8

5 Take a pencil and mark the position of all the pilot holes to be drilled. First measure and mark a point 2½ inches (6cm) in from each end of the wall plates, *outside* the rectangle representing the bracket. Then mark a point 2 inches (5cm) in from each end *inside* the penciled rectangle on the plates. On the canopy shelf, mark a point 1 inch (2.5cm) in from each end of the rectangles that represent the brackets.

6 Using an ⅛-inch (3-mm) drill bit, drill through each point marked in Step 5, clamping each piece as you go. Next, clamp a bracket in a vertical position using a workbench or a vise. Center a wall plate on the bracket and use the drill to go back through the holes on the wall plate to make a secondary hole in the bracket. Do the same for the other bracket.

7 Now countersink all the holes you have made, making sure that you countersink the correct side of each hole. For the wall plates, countersink the holes within the marked-out rectangle on the side that attaches to the wall. The other two holes, which fix the shelf to the wall, should be countersunk on the other side. Countersink the holes that join the shelf to the bracket on the side that will be the top of the shelf (see below).

8 To assemble the shelf, join the wall plates to the brackets. Screw the No.8 screws through the two holes in the center of each wall plate until their tips are visible at the other side. Line the screw tips up with the holes in the brackets and screw them in the rest of the way. Repeat this process when joining the canopy shelf to the brackets. For extra strength you can use wood glue along all the joints.

PROFESSIONAL TIP

When countersinking pilot holes, make sure that the countersinks are deep enough for the screwheads to be below the surface of the MDF. This will allow the shelf brackets to fit flush against the wall. When joining two pieces of marked-up wood, it is easier not to attempt to line up all the marks before joining the parts. Loosely secure the two pieces at one end so that they are held in place while you line up and loosely secure the other end. Once the two pieces are correctly lined up, drive the screws in fully.

PUTTING IT TOGETHER ~ STEPS 9 TO 12

9 If you wish, sand the edges smooth with sandpaper and wipe away the dust with a damp cloth. Protect your work surface with a drop cloth or newspaper and paint the canopy shelf and supports, preferably in the same color as the wall so that it recedes into the background. If you use a matte water-base paint, it should dry in about an hour. If you wish, you can use a gloss paint but it will take longer to dry.

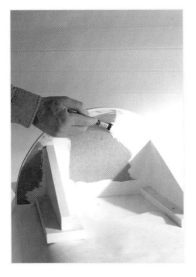

10 The canopy shelf must be centered on the wall above the bed. Use a tape measure to find the center point of your bed and mark this point with a thumbtack or small object. Dangle a plumbline (or string and key) from the desired shelf height until it points directly at your mark. This will be the center point of the shelf. Mark the wall at this point with pencil.

11 To attach the shelf to the wall, find the center of the shelf and line it up with the pencil mark on the wall. Before securing it, use a carpenter's level to make sure it is straight. Attach the wall plates to the wall with a No.8 screw in each of the remaining pilot holes. Depending on the type of wall you have, you may need to add wall anchors.

12 Prepare the fabric as described in the box below. Then mark the fabric in half along its longest side with dressmaker's chalk or crayon and cut it in half with sharp scissors. If you do not have chalk or crayon, carefully fold the fabric in half along its longest side and cut the fabric on the fold.

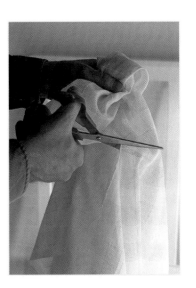

PREPARING THE FABRIC

It is a good idea to dry-clean and iron your fabric before attaching it to the shelf for the first time. When ironing delicate fabrics, keep the iron at a cool setting to avoid damaging the material. If the lengths of fabric need to be cleaned, the staples can be removed using staple removers. However, care will have to be taken not to tear the fabric when removing the staples, and, of course, Steps 13 to 16 will need to be repeated when it is time to fit the fabric into position again.

FINISHING IT OFF – STEPS 13 TO 16

13 Take one piece of fabric and fold it back 3 inches (7.5cm) along its length (to tuck behind the shelf). Then fold over about 2 feet (60cm) to the front, across its width (for the flounce). Place the folded edge of the fabric against the edge of the shelf near one wall and staple the fabric to the shelf. (Make sure the fabric for the flounce is facing you.) Leave about 1 ft (30cm) of fabric, then staple it just past the center of the shelf.

14 The end of the fabric should be stapled at the end of the shelf, close to the wall. Continue stapling the center of each loose piece of fabric to the edge of the shelf. You should use about nine staples to attach this piece of fabric and the staples should be evenly positioned at about 2½-inch (6-cm) intervals.

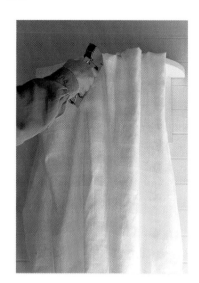

15 To make the flounce, fold the extra 2 feet (60cm) of fabric back on itself and staple it just over the top of the shelf. You should aim to staple it over the top of the existing staples. This will hide the staples beneath.

16 Repeat Steps 12 to 15 with the other piece of fabric, starting from the other end of the shelf: don't forget to tuck the 3-inch (7.5-cm) excess behind the canopy shelf. Fold the existing flounce out of the way, on the top of the shelf. Staple the second flounce in place and fluff out the material.

FINISHING OFF THE CANOPY

There are various ways of arranging and finishing off the bed canopy. The flounce of the fabric can be puffed up to create a cloudy effect and the sides of the fabric can be tied back with curtain ties, or left to hang loosely around the sides of the bed. Different color braiding can also be glued along the edge of the shelf at the top of the flounce to give it a decorative finish. If you feel really inspired, try adding a tassel or two: these also come in a wide range of shapes and sizes.

BATHROOM FLOOR

For a practical and low-maintenance bathroom floor that's never cold under bare feet, you can't do better than vinyl tiles. We've added a simple border design and finished off the floor with a vinyl-tiled baseboard.

TOOLS

Electric sander

Plane

Hammer

Putty knife

Nail set

Utility knife

Tape measure

Metal ruler

Cutting mat or alternative

Thick sponge

C-clamp

Workbench

MATERIALS

❖ Hardboard (Masonite), see below

❖ Vinyl tiles in main floor color

❖ Vinyl tiles in border color

❖ Floor adhesive and applicator

❖ Annular ring nails, 1 inch (2.5cm) long

❖ Quick-drying filler

VARIATION

❖ As above, with more vinyl tiles in main floor color

NOTE

Multiply the length by the width of the room to work out the area of the floor you are covering. You will then need to check that you have enough hardboard, vinyl tiles, and floor adhesive. The manufacturer will usually specify how much coverage you will get. Make sure you allow for error and buy about 5 percent more tiles than you need.

STARTING OUT – STEPS 1 TO 4

1 To prepare your floor for tiling, use a hammer and nail set to drive in any nail heads that are protruding from the floor. It is important that the surface is even because any imperfections in the floor will create an uneven finish.

2 In order to create a perfectly flat surface to work on, you will need to cover the floor with hardboard. Lay the hardboard so that the joints are staggered and do not align. You will probably need to cut some of the board: use a metal ruler and a utility knife to cut the sheets. Make sure you lay the hardboard rough-side-up.

3 When the hardboard is in place you may find that it is slightly warped. To flatten it, apply water to the surface of the board with a sponge. Once the hardboard has absorbed the water, it will begin to flatten.

4 Secure the hardboard into place with annular ring nails. These nails are designed to grip the floorboards and will ensure that the hardboard is securely fixed into position. The nails should be positioned at 6-inch (15-cm) intervals all over the hardboard in a grid pattern.

PROFESSIONAL TIP

You may find that there are gaps between some of the joints of the hardboard you have placed into position, especially if you have not been precise in measuring and cutting the hardboard. This will not matter as any gaps can be filled using filler. It is important, however, to ensure that all the gaps are filled to prevent the tiles from sinking. When nailing the hardboard to the floor, you may wish to mark out rows to form a grid pattern to ensure accuracy.

PUTTING IT TOGETHER - STEPS 5 TO 8

5 Apply quick-drying filler over each nail head on the hardboard. When the filler has dried, sand the whole area with an electric sander to create a smooth surface. This step is very important; it ensures a smooth surface on which to lay your tiles, preventing any area of the tiled floor from sinking. Use a damp sponge to wipe away the dust left behind after sanding.

6 Use a tape measure to measure along the first side of your room. Divide this measurement by the length of one tile to figure out how many tiles you need. The tiles on the outer border are half-tiles and the colored border is made up of quarter-tiles. If you need to plan the floor pattern, do this now (see below).

7 To make half-tiles for the outer border, place a tile on a flat surface and find the center of one side. Mark it with a sharp utility knife then repeat on the opposite edge of the tile. (The utility knife will provide a much more accurate mark than a pencil.) Score the tile several times, making sure you protect your work surface. When you have scored enough tiles, follow the instructions in Step 9 to snap them in half.

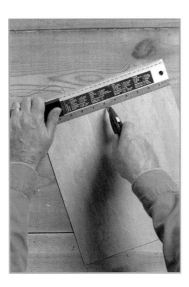

8 To make the quarter-tiles for the border, cut the tiles in half as before. Then divide each half again to form four equal tiles. Use a sharp utility knife to score the tile several times but do not apply too much pressure on the knife because this may cause the blade to slip. Repeat until you have scored the amount of quarter-tiles needed.

PLANNING THE FLOOR

If your walls are not straight, your border will not be straight, so spend some time planning your floor. This way you can also avoid having to cut tiles to fit later on. Carefully measure the floor and figure out how much space the full-tiles and the quarter-tile border will take. Then figure out what size to cut the outer border tiles. If you don't have time for complicated measuring and your walls are relatively straight, filling the border with diagonally laid tiles is a quick and easy way to cover the floor.

PUTTING IT TOGETHER – STEPS 9 TO 12

9 To break a scored tile, hold a tile in both hands and snap it along the scored lines you have made. If you have scored the tiles sufficiently, they will break easily. Dividing the tiles in this way produces a neat, straight line.

10 Now take five or six of the quarter-size tiles and clamp them all together on a workbench or in a vise. Set a well-sharpened plane to take off a minimum amount of material, and run it along the length of the tiles to ensure that they are all exactly the same size. Repeat until all the quarter tiles and the half-size tiles are planed. Planing the tiles will help avoid gaps in the floor when they are fitted.

11 Position a half-tile up against the baseboard, then place a quarter-tile next to it. Mark the width of the two tiles on the hardboard in pencil. Repeat at intervals around the room and connect the pencil marks to form a border. Dilute the flooring adhesive, adding four parts water to one part adhesive and apply it within the pencil lines. Comb through the adhesive with the toothed end of a spreader.

12 To form the outer border lay down one half-tile at a time, positioning it neatly up against the baseboard along one side of the room. Butt the tiles against each other and press them down firmly into position. If adhesive squeezes through between the tiles, it can be wiped off when all the tiles are fitted.

PROFESSIONAL TIP

When you apply the flooring adhesive to your floor, you may find that the adhesive dries very quickly. The more porous your floor is, the quicker the adhesive will dry. If this is the case, dilute the adhesive by adding a considerable amount of water to a small amount of the adhesive. This will slow down the drying process. The mixture can then be spread over the area you are working on and the tiles laid on top of it. Use the toothed end of the spreader to comb through the adhesive.

FINISHING IT OFF – STEPS 13 TO 16

13 At the end of the first row of tiles you will probably have to cut a tile to fit. Hold a tile against the edge of the baseboard, and use a utility knife to mark the width of tile needed to complete the row. Use a metal ruler and utility knife to measure and cut the tile to the size required and then press the piece firmly into position on the adhesive. Continue fitting the outer border tiles all around the room.

14 Lay the quarter-tiles for the inner border against the half-tiles. When you have reached the end of the first row, position another quarter-tile at right angles to the row and cut the last tile fitted to allow for the width of this quarter-tile. Continue to fit all the border tiles around the room, working on one side of the floor at a time.

15 Once you have completed your border pattern, use full-size tiles to fill in the center of your floor. Apply adhesive to small areas at a time, and measure and cut any tiles needed to fill the gaps, unless you have planned the floor pattern to avoid this (see tip box page 70). Continue laying tiles until the whole floor is completely covered.

16 Wipe over the surface of the floor with a damp sponge and remove any adhesive that has squeezed through the joints between the tiles. The flooring adhesive you have used will permanently bond the vinyl tiles to the floor.

THE BEAUTY OF VINYL

The vinyl tiles used on this project are low-cost tiles that are also hard wearing and easy to clean. The tiles are waterproof and therefore ideal for use in a bathroom or kitchen. Vinyl tiles are available in a wide range of colors and finishes and, unlike ceramic tiles, they do not create a cold floor. The tiles are flexible and can be cut, making them ideal for fitting around awkward corners or sink pedestals. They are also perfect for arranging in different patterns on the floor.

VARIATION - VINYL BASEBOARD

1 For a more unusual finish for your vinyl floor, add vinyl to the baseboard. To figure out what size to cut the tiles, hold a tile against the baseboard and mark it on either side of the tile, at the point where the molding begins on the baseboard.

2 Score the tiles and then snap them as shown before. Clamp the tiles all together and plane them as before, so that they are all an equal size. Sand down one of the edges so that when the tile is laid, the uppermost edge will have a smooth finish.

3 Apply adhesive directly onto each tile, without diluting it, and press each tile against the baseboard. Make sure you comb the adhesive on the tile and work on a small area at a time.

4 Wipe over the vinyl with a damp sponge to remove any adhesive that squeezed through the joints in the tiles. Be careful not to knock the baseboard until the adhesive has dried.

RECYCLING OLD TILES

There is no need to buy brand new vinyl tiles for this project. If you already have old tiles that you particularly like, you can reuse them. However, they are likely to have a layer of old adhesive on the back of them that will need to be removed before the tiles can be laid down. In order to remove the adhesive, soak the tiles in warm water for half an hour. This will loosen much of the adhesive and allow you to scrape it off. This should be done while the tiles are still wet. Once they are cleaned, you can use them.

WINDOW SHUTTERS

Add a touch of continental Europe to your home with some simple internal wooden shutters. A decorative wooden frame makes them a particularly striking feature. Both pretty and practical, they keep rooms cool in summer and cozy in winter.

TOOLS

Paintbrush

Putty knife

Hand screwdriver

⅛-inch (3-mm) drill bit

Pencil

Countersink bit

Power drill/ Screwdriver

Awl

C-clamp

Damp cloth

Tape measure

Hand saw

Long ruler or length of batten

Sandpaper

MATERIALS

For a 3- x 3-feet (90- x 90-cm) window jamb:

❖ Two shutter doors to fit the window reveal or larger

❖ 10 feet (3m) of 1 x 2-inch (2.5 x 5-cm) wood

❖ No. 8 screws, 1¾ inches (4.5cm) long

❖ Piece of scrap cardboard

❖ 4 flush-mount hinges and screws

❖ Sliding bolt and screws

❖ Hook and latch and screws

❖ Door latch and screws

❖ Wall anchors, optional

❖ Quick-drying filler (wood-colored optional)

❖ Gloss paint, one-coat paint, or matte varnish

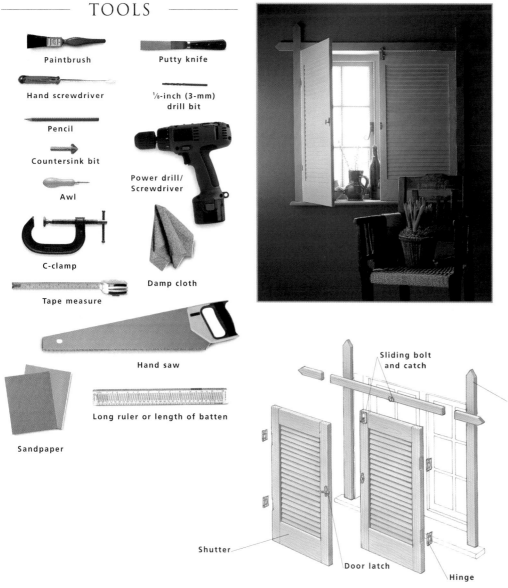

Sliding bolt and catch

long batten

Shutter

Door latch

Hinge

NOTE

The shutters can go inside the window jamb or sit outside the jamb; it is a matter of taste. If your window is larger than 3 x 3 feet (90 x 90cm), you will also need to allow for more wood batten.

STARTING OUT – STEPS 1 TO 4

1 Measure along the top of the jamb and mark the center point in pencil. The distance between the edge of the jamb and this point is the width of each shutter. Then measure the height of the jamb to give you the length of each shutter.

2 If you need to cut the shutters to the correct size, transfer the measurements taken in Step 1 onto each shutter, allowing a ⅟₁₆-inch (1.5-mm) gap between them for movement. Cut off equal amounts on both sides to ensure the shutters look even. If you don't have a very long ruler to mark your cutting line, use a long piece of batten to help you.

3 Position the first shutter on your work surface and hold it firmly in position, or use a clamp. Line your saw up with the marked lines and cut it to the dimensions required. Repeat with the second shutter.

4 Position a long piece of batten next to the jamb. Mark the edge of the batten at the point where it meets the top of the jamb. Draw a line across the batten 6 inches (15cm) above this mark. For accuracy, measure and mark the second piece of batten on the other side of the jamb, as the measurements may differ slightly.

FRAMING THE SHUTTERS

If your shutters are larger than your jamb, they will ideally need to be cut to size. The battens that frame the jamb should also be set flush with the jamb for a neater finish. However, the advantage of having a frame is that it can be set back from the edge of the jamb to accommodate the size of your shutters, eliminating the need to cut them to size. Using the frame in this way also allows the doors to be attached to wood rather than to the jamb, which in some cases may be made of plaster.

PUTTING IT TOGETHER - STEPS 5 TO 8

5 You need to cut the end to a point with its tip on the line you have just drawn. Measure and mark the midpoint of the line, then draw two diagonal lines from this point to the edge of the batten, 1 inch (2.5cm) away. Clamp the batten to your workbench and cut out the point. Then cut the second batten in the same way.

6 Using a ⅛-inch (3-mm) drill bit, drill and countersink holes at 12-inch (30-cm) intervals along each vertical batten. Position a length of batten so that it is flush with the side of the jamb and mark the wall through the holes with an awl. Drill into the wall at the awl marks and add wall anchors if necessary. Screw the batten into place using the no.8 screws. Repeat on the other side of the window.

7 Hold a piece of batten along the top of the jamb between the two vertical battens. Use a pencil to mark the horizontal batten at both ends, at the points where it meets the inside edge of each vertical batten. Draw a straight line across the batten at these points and then cut the horizontal batten to length. Drill pilot holes in the batten and attach it to the wall following the instructions in Step 6.

8 Take a small piece of batten and shape the ends to a point, as in Step 5. Position it on top of the vertical batten already attached to the wall. Mark the side of the batten at the point where it meets the top edge of the horizontal batten. Draw a line across the small piece of batten at this point and cut it with a saw. Measure and cut another piece of batten for the other horizontal batten.

TAKING MEASUREMENTS

A lockable tape measure is the handiest measuring tool for taking most of the measurements required in this project. However, if you have a good eye and are confident, you may not always find that it is strictly necessary to use a tape measure or a ruler to take measurements. In some instances, it is actually better to use a piece of wood and take measurements from the work you already have in position as you go along. This will ensure that you get a neat and accurate fit.

PUTTING IT TOGETHER - STEPS 9 TO 12

9 Attach each small piece of pointed batten to the wall, following the instructions given in Step 6. One screw will be sufficient to hold each piece of wood in place. It should be positioned so that it appears to be a continuation of the horizontal batten.

10 Measure the length of the shutters and mark the position of each hinge on the outside edge; attach the inner part of the hinge with the screws provided. The barrel of the hinge sits flush against the front of the shutter and the inner section of the hinge should be fitted to the door so that the countersunk holes face upward.

11 Position the first shutter in the jamb, sitting it on a piece of cardboard to lift it up slightly. (The shutters need to sit slightly higher than the window ledge when hung to allow them to move.) Use a pencil to mark the position of the top of each hinge on the vertical batten. Remove the shutter and repeat this process with the other shutter on the opposite jamb.

12 Now position the shutter flat against the wall as though it were fully open. Then fold back the outer part of each hinge until it is flat against the inside edge of the vertical batten. Align the top of each hinge with the pencil line on the batten and check that the countersink is facing outward. Screw each hinge into place with a screwdriver. Repeat with the other shutter.

PROFESSIONAL TIP

Flush-mount hinges do away with the need to chisel and recess the doors and battens; and they also allow the shutters to open fully. If you have decorative molding around your window, you will either need to remove it in order to fit your shutters, or keep it and use a different type of hinge called a parliament hinge. This hinge allows for the thickness of the molding but will need to be fitted using a different technique and will require the assistance of a carpenter.

FINISHING IT OFF – STEPS 13 TO 16

13 To keep the shutters open, attach a hook and latch to each shutter. With the shutter flat against the wall, mark a point 2 inches (5cm) up from the outermost bottom corner. Attach the eye at this point, using small screws to fit. Place the hook into the eye to establish the position of the hook plate on the wall. Secure the hook plate to the wall and then repeat the process with the other shutter.

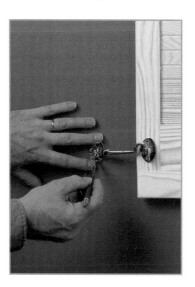

14 Now fit one of the shutters with a sliding bolt. If you have a choice, fit it to the one in front of a nonopening window. Attach the bolt on the front of the shutter on the vertical panel at the top inner corner. Then slide the bolt into the eye. Mark the correct position of the eye on the horizontal batten and attach it to the batten with screws.

15 The shutters are kept closed with a door latch. Measure and mark halfway down the length of one of the shutters. Attach the latch so that it is flush with the central edge of the shutter. Put the latch onto the keep plate and mark the correct position of the keep plate on the edge of the opposite door. Then screw the plate in place.

16 Cover all screws with quick-drying filler. (If you do not intend to paint the battens, use a wood-colored filler.) When the filler has dried, smooth down the surface of the wood with sandpaper and use a damp cloth to wipe off the residue. Then either varnish the frame and shutters or paint them in a color that suits your room.

PROFESSIONAL TIP

The advantage of attaching all the hardware to the doors before painting them is that the paint will not be at risk of being damaged when you fit them. The fittings can all be removed when it is time to paint the doors, and reattached again when the doors are dry. When painting shutters, be careful not to apply too much paint along the two center lengths of the doors because this will close up the gap between the doors slightly and may prevent them from opening easily.

WINDOW DRESSING

*Make the most of the windows in your home: installing a roller blind is a stylish,
simple, practical solution that shows off the windowsill. For a more opulent look, add
a formal valance and easy-to-hang unlined curtains.*

TOOLS

Scissors

Power drill/
Screwdriver

Iron

Staple gun

Hammer

Masking tape   C-clamp   Jigsaw

Metal file

Tape measure   Small hacksaw

Metal ruler   Awl (optional)

Screwdriver   ⅛-inch (3-mm)
drill bit

Countersink bit   ¼-inch (6-mm)
drill bit

Marker pen

Craft knife

Cutting mat

Pencil

Workbench (optional)

MATERIALS

❖ Roller blind to fit the window or larger

❖ Roller blind brackets and screws to fit

❖ Piece of scrap wood

❖ Wall anchors (optional)

VARIATION

For a window measuring 3 x 3 feet (90 x 90cm):

❖ Piece of ¾ x 6-inch (2 x 10cm) soft wood,
4½ feet (1.5m) long

❖ Hardboard (Masonite), 6 by 42 inches
(15 by 105cm)

❖ Hardboard finishing nails, 1 inch (2.5cm) long

❖ Glazed chintz fabric, 4½ feet (1.5m) long

❖ P.V.A. (white) glue

❖ Braid, 4½ feet (1.5m) long

❖ Pincer curtain clips

❖ Two wall-mirror fixing plates

❖ Wall anchors (optional)

❖ No. 8 screws, 1¾ inches (4.5cm) long

❖ Voile fabric, 4 feet (1.2m) wide, 12 feet
(3.6m) long

❖ Adhesive hemming tape

❖ Curtain pole and fixing plates (with screws)

STARTING OUT – STEPS 1 TO 4

1 To cut the roller blind to size, hold it up across the width of the jamb with one end of it inside the jamb. Measure the excess and note how much you will have to cut off the blind to make it fit neatly inside the jamb. Now measure the drop of your jamb and add 6 inches (15cm) to this measurement. (If you don't intend to add curtains you can place the blind outside the window jamb.)

2 Remove the pole from your blind and lay the blind on a cutting mat on a flat surface. Mark the correct width (taken in Step 1) at intervals along the length of the blind. Use a ruler and a sharp craft knife to cut the blind down to the correct width. Check the length of the blind and cut it to the length figured out in Step 1.

3 Remove the plastic lath that sits across the bottom of the blind and position it on your work surface with a piece of scrap wood beneath it. Using a small hacksaw, cut the lath down to the same width as the blind. Hold the lath firmly in position when sawing to ensure a straight cut.

4 Transfer the width measurement of the blind to the metal tube, using a marker pen. Position the tube on your workbench and, once again, use a small hacksaw to cut the tube to the same width as the blind. Use a metal file to smooth off any sharp edges on the cut pole.

PROFESSIONAL TIP

When reassembling the blind, the metal pole must be squared up to the edge of the blind. This will ensure that when the blind is rolled up and down, it will be straight. Therefore, accuracy in cutting is essential for a straight blind. Do not use scissors to cut the fabric of the blind as this will not be accurate enough. For best results use a craft knife with a sharp blade and a ruler at all times to guide the cut. When working with a craft knife, keep your free hand clear of the blade and use a cutting mat to protect your work surface.

PUTTING IT TOGETHER – STEPS 5 TO 8

5 Peel back the protective strip of paper along the length of the pole to expose a sticky strip. Line up the cut width-edge of the blind with the edge of the sticky strip and stick the blind firmly onto the pole. Make sure that the blind is pressed down exactly in line with the edge of the strip, otherwise it will not roll up and down evenly.

6 Fit the brackets that hold the blind to the inside top corners of the jamb. Hold each bracket against the wooden frame at either side of the window and drill through the holes on the brackets into the wooden frame. Secure the brackets into position with the screws provided.

7 Reassemble the blind, placing the lath back through the base and adding the end stops to the pole. Click the chain attachment into place, ensuring that it sits on the left side of the pole. Fit your blind onto the brackets by sliding the side with the chain attachment into position first, then slide the other side into position. The fixings should click into place, securing the blind.

8 The length of the chain or cord will also need to be adjusted to fit the height of your jamb. Cut the chain or cord so that, when the curtain is fully extended, it sits just above the windowsill.

KEEPING THE BLIND STRAIGHT

If you find that the blind is not hanging straight once it is in position, unwind it all the way and stick a few layers of masking tape on the pole. If the blind is dropping to the left, add the masking tape to the left-hand side of the pole. If it is dropping to the right, add tape to the right-hand side. The layers of masking tape add an extra thickness at one end of the blind, thereby correcting the balance. If the blind is still uneven, continue to add layers of tape until the balance is perfect.

VARIATION – ADDING A VALANCE AND CURTAINS

1 Measure the width of the jamb and add 6 inches (15cm) to this figure; in this case 42 inches (105cm). This is the length of the top piece of the valance, which should be cut from the 6-inch (15-cm) wide pine. The two side pieces (also made from pine) measure 4 x 6 inches (10 x 15cm) each. The front piece is 1½ inches (4cm) (which is two widths of wood) shorter than the top piece, and should be cut from the 6-inch (15-cm) wide hardboard.

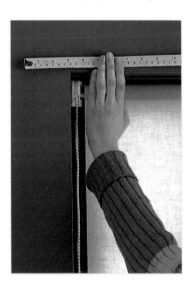

2 Cut out all the pieces with a jigsaw. To shape the front of the valance, draw a line 1½ inches (3.75cm) in from one of the long sides. Mark a cut-off point 6 inches (15cm) from either end, then draw a diagonal from the edge of the hardboard to the penciled line. Clamp the board to your workbench and cut out the area with a jigsaw.

3 To assemble the valance, drill and countersink two evenly-spaced pilot holes ⅜ inch (1cm) in from one of the 6-inch (15-cm) sides on each of the side pieces. Join the two sides to the top piece with a No.8 screw in each pilot hole. Next, attach the front piece to the top and sides with finishing nails placed at 6-inch (15-cm) intervals.

4 Position the valance in the center of the chintz and check that the fabric will cover each side. Fold the fabric over one short side of the valance and staple it on the inside, placing the staples at roughly 3-inch (7.5-cm) intervals. Pull the fabric taut from the opposite end and staple it down in the same way. Fold the fabric over the other edges, pulling the fabric taut and stapling it as you work, until all the valance is covered.

PROFESSIONAL TIP

To make a neatly covered valance, the fabric you use should be ironed to eliminate any creases. When ironing, make sure the iron is at the correct temperature for the type of fabric to avoid damaging it in any way. When folding the fabric over the top of the valance, it does not matter if the fabric overlaps, particularly at the corners. The top of the valance will be out of sight once it is fixed into place, so make sure any folds at the corners are on the top, not at the sides.

PUTTING IT TOGETHER – STEPS 5 TO 8

5 Now apply a layer of P.V.A. glue along the bottom inside edges of the hardboard and fold the excess material over. At each corner, make a small snip in the fabric to allow you to fold the fabric over. Make sure the snips are away from the edge of the hardboard to avoid exposing any of the board. Press the fabric firmly onto the glue.

6 Attach the braid along the front of the valance using P.V.A. glue. To fit it around corners, cut the ribbon, leaving enough to fold over at the points where the direction of the valance changes. This forms a pocket in which the ends of the main length of braid can be inserted. Attach braid around the sides of the valance. Fold the ends of the braid under or around the back of the valance and glue down.

7 Using a small hacksaw, cut the curtain pole to the length of the inside of the valance. Slide a curtain clip onto the pole and tape it in the center of the pole with masking tape. This will prevent other clips from sliding down the pole and getting in the way when attaching the pole to the valance. Slide on the rest of the curtain clips, making sure that you use an even number.

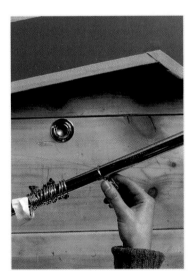

8 Attach one of the mounting plates to the inside of one end of the valance. Position it 1 inch (2.5cm) down from the top piece of the valance and 1 inch (2.5cm) in from the back. Slip one end of the pole into the fixed mounting plate, slide the other mounting plate onto the pole and position it on the other end of the valance. Then screw the second plate in position.

DECORATIVE VALANCES

The valance in this project is fairly formal and restrained with its simple braid edging. However, there is no reason why you should not make a much bolder statement with the valance, covering it in a jazzy stripe, an eye-catching check, or a sizzling colored silk.

Depending on the fabric chosen, decorate the valance with luxurious long silk fringing or tassels. Stitch on pretty satin bows in a contrasting color or sew on scattered multicolored glass beads that will reflect the light.

FINISHING IT OFF – STEPS 9 TO 12

9 Measure 6 inches (15cm) in from each end of the valance and mark the positions of the two wall mirror plates to be attached to the back edge of the valance. Use a screwdriver to attach the plates firmly in position.

10 Center the valance across the jamb and mark the position of one of the mirror plates on the wall. Drill a hole where you have marked the wall and place a wall anchor into the hole if necessary. Attach one side of the valance to the wall with No.8 screws. Before attaching the other side in the same way, use a carpenter's level to check that the valance is straight.

11 Use a voile or similar lightweight fabric for the floor-length curtains. Cut the fabric so that you have two pieces measuring 4 x 6 feet (1.2 x 1.8m). Turn 1-inch (2.5-cm) hems on the top and bottom of each piece, using an iron to press the folds in position.

12 Use adhesive hemming tape to hold the hems in place. (You can sew them if you have a sewing machine.) Line up a strip of hemming tape along the edge of the first fold. Turn the folded fabric over another 1 inch (2.5cm) over the hemming tape, and iron the hem down. Make the other hems the same way. Attach the curtains at each end of the valance with pincer curtain clips.

CURTAIN FABRICS

If you wish to use a heavier fabric to make the curtains, or would like to make more of a feature of the pelmet, you will need to make the pelmet larger. In this project, the pelmet extends 3 inches (7.5cm) on either side of the window jamb and 4 inches (10cm) away from the wall. The delicate fabric used for each curtain will fit into this space when gathered up. If you are using thicker curtains, you will need to measure farther out on each side of the jamb and farther away from the wall to accommodate the thickness of the heavier material.

CEILING TREATMENT

Enliven a room with a molded cornice that helps smooth the transition between the wall and the ceiling. Cornices come in a wide variety of molding shapes and sizes, so don't limit yourself to the plainest one.

TOOLS

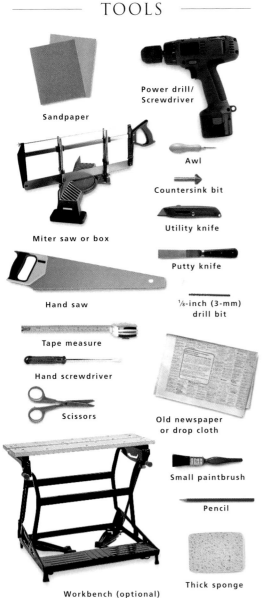

Sandpaper

Power drill/ Screwdriver

Awl

Countersink bit

Miter saw or box

Utility knife

Hand saw

Putty knife

⅛-inch (3-mm) drill bit

Tape measure

Hand screwdriver

Scissors

Old newspaper or drop cloth

Workbench (optional)

Small paintbrush

Pencil

Thick sponge

MATERIALS

❖ Plaster cornice (see below)

❖ Small piece of cardboard to use as a guide

❖ P.V.A. (white) glue

❖ Quick-drying powder adhesive and bucket for mixing

❖ Piece of scrap wood

❖ Old tile

❖ Quick-drying filler

❖ Small pot of water-base paint

VARIATION

❖ Plaster ceiling rose

❖ Piece of scrap cardboard, at least as large as the ceiling rose

❖ No. 8 screws, 1¾ inches (4.5cm) long

❖ Powder adhesive and applicator

❖ Quick-drying filler

❖ White water-base paint

NOTES

To figure out how much cornice you need to buy, measure each wall and add the lengths together to determine the perimeter of the room. Allow for error and buy slightly more than you need.

When fitting a ceiling rose, turn off the electricity at the main box before starting.

STARTING OUT – STEPS 1 TO 4

1 Measure the precise length of the first wall you are working on, taking your measure right into the corners at each end. Then mark the required length of cornice.

2 Protect the floor beneath your work area with a drop cloth: cutting plaster produces a lot of white dust. Protect the work surface itself by resting the cornice on a piece of scrap wood. Cut the miter with an old saw (see below). To work out which way to cut the miter see the diagram on page 110.

3 Cut a piece of cardboard to the width of the cornice and use it to mark a pencil line along the wall, indicating the depth of the cornice from the ceiling. This guideline outlines the area you need to prepare for the adhesive, as well as providing a guide for positioning the cornice.

4 To help the adhesive bond to the wall, you need to prepare the wall surface. Working about 1 inch (2.5cm) above the pencil line, use a utility knife to scratch crisscross lines along the entire length of the wall.

PROFESSIONAL TIP

When buying a cornice ask for the correct miter cutter to fit the particular style you have chosen. Some lumberyards, mail-order suppliers, and home building centers will also provide a miter pattern with the molding, as well as instructions about how to fit the molding to your wall edge. Use an old saw, if you have one, when cutting your lengths of cornice to size. Cutting through plaster can quickly blunt saw blades and it is not worth risking damage to a new blade by using it for this task.

PUTTING IT TOGETHER – STEPS 5 TO 8

5 In order to prevent the raw plaster from absorbing too much moisture from the adhesive, which would weaken the bond between the cornice and the wall, brush the area you have scored with P.V.A. Slightly dilute the P.V.A. first, but do not over-dilute it: it should be of a non-drip consistency.

6 If you are using powder adhesive, make the adhesive following the manufacturer's instructions. Apply adhesive liberally to both the side and edges of the cornice that will come into contact with the wall and ceiling. (You may find a putty knife useful for this.)

7 Take the length of cornice and line up the "wall edge" with the pencil line. Push the "ceiling edge" back until it sits neatly against the ceiling. Press the cornice firmly to the wall all along its length. Don't worry if the adhesive squeezes out over the edges; it can be removed easily (see next step).

8 Excess adhesive will probably come through the top and bottom of the cornice. Use a putty knife to remove it, running the knife along the top and bottom edges and removing about 4 inches (10cm) at a time. Scrape the adhesive off the putty knife onto an old tile.

CONCEALING CABLES AND WIRES

Some cornices have a hollow channel on the back, running along the full length of the molding. Its purpose is to conceal any cables and wires that need to be run along the top of the wall. Feed wires or cables through the cornice before fixing it in position.

Peel back the paper covering the channel and use a draw wire to pull the more flexible wire or cable through the gap. A draw wire is a nylon wire that stays rigid and can therefore be easily fed through the channel.

PUTTING IT TOGETHER ~ STEPS 9 TO 12

9 Make sure there are no gaps between the cornice and the wall. (If there are, simply add more adhesive.) Use a damp sponge to clean any excess adhesive off the wall. It is also important to remove all traces of adhesive from the surface of the cornice before it dries. The only way to remove dried adhesive is by chipping it off, which would damage the surface.

10 Repeat the procedure from Steps 1 to 9 for fitting the next piece of cornice, carefully measuring the length from corner to corner. Butt the corners together using both hands to slide the cornice firmly into place.

11 If the wall is very long, it may be easier to work with two pieces of cornice, joining them in the middle. This middle joint, like those at the ends, should be a miter joint, which is neater than a straight cut.

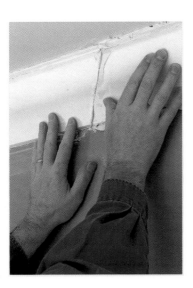

12 For a small section of the wall (for example, around a chimney jog) you can use a suitable length of cornice to take your measurement rather than a tape measure. Take a piece of cornice that already has an internal miter at one end (see page 110). Hold it up so that the point of the internal miter is touching the wall and measure and mark the cornice at the edge of the external corner.

CUTTING AND FITTING

Each piece of molding should be measured and cut as you progress to ensure accuracy and to allow for slight differences in the lengths of the walls. Once you have cut a piece of molding to size, place it in the corner and trim the ends as appropriate. By working in this way, you will ensure neat and accurate corner fittings. Cutting each piece as you go along is also useful since cutting one internal miter leaves an external miter ready to be used to fit another wall.

FINISHING IT OFF – STEPS 13 TO 16

13 To butt up the mitered edges, line up the two pieces of cornice along the pencil guideline you made in Step 3. Ease the lengths of cornice into place so that the edges align and fit neatly together. Use the adhesive as a filler if the edges do not fit exactly.

14 In some cases, the cornice will need a stop to make way for pipes or a stairwell. If possible, use a length of cornice with an external miter, or miter it to fit onto the edge of your fitted cornice. Use an adjustable rule to mark a straight line on the front of the piece. The line should be taken from the point of the external miter and straight down.

15 Cut through the cornice, being as accurate as possible. It is better to cut through the piece face-up as it will prevent the front of the cornice from fraying along the cut. Add adhesive to the squared-off piece to form a neat corner. Again, use adhesive to fill any gaps and wipe down with a damp sponge to remove any excess adhesive.

16 Finally, paint the cornice with one or two coats of matte water-base paint, either in plain white or in a color that complements your wall color.

KEEPING IT CLEAN

Lay drop cloths to protect your floors from the fine white powder released when cutting plaster. Drop cloths will also protect your carpets against drops of adhesive. If adhesive does get onto the carpet, let it dry before attempting to remove it. It sits on top of the carpet and can be easily picked off when dry. If you attempt to remove adhesive while it is wet, you will embed it further into the carpet. You will then need to seek professional advice on how to remove it.

VARIATION – ADDING A CEILING ROSE

1 Turn off the electricity at the main box and remove your light fixture. Then, trace around the ceiling rose on a piece of cardboard and cut this out with scissors. Make a hole in the center of the cardboard and hold it in position on the ceiling, pulling the wire through. Locate a stud (see below) and punch two holes through the cardboard with an awl, on either side of the central hole and following the postion of the studs.

2 Place the cardboard on top of the ceiling rose. Mark the position of the holes in the cardboard on the front of the rose using a pencil. Drill a pilot hole at each of the positions marked and countersink each pilot hole.

3 Turn the rose over and spread a liberal amount of all-purpose adhesive on the back. Comb the adhesive to help it bond to the ceiling and make sure that the central hole is left clear for the electric wire to feed through. Apply sufficient adhesive around the edges of the rose so you do not need to fill any gaps once it is in position.

4 Feed the wire through the hole, and press the rose firmly onto the ceiling. Use two screws to secure it in position. (Do not drive the screws in too tightly; this may crack the molding.) Remove any adhesive that has squeezed out around the edges with a putty knife and a damp sponge. Finally, cover the screw heads with quick-drying filler and lightly sand them down when the filler has dried.

LOCATING STUDS

Studs always run in the opposite direction of the floorboards. Check the floorboards on the floor above to determine the direction. Another way to locate a stud is to knock on the ceiling. If it sounds dull, you have found one. Once you have found a stud and marked the position of the first hole, position the next hole on the other side of the central one. If you make a mistake, don't worry; holes drilled in the ceiling will be covered by the rose itself. Just be careful not to screw into any electric wires.

PAINT EFFECTS

There's nothing like a lick of paint to breathe new life into tired old walls. Decorate your room with flourish using one of these paint effects. Begin with the simple technique of sponging; when you build up your confidence, try your hand at marbling.

TOOLS

Large bowl or paint can & stick for mixing

Badgerhair brush

Medium-size paintbrush

Several plates or saucers

Natural sea sponge

No. 3 sable paintbrush

MATERIALS

❖ Water-base paint in blue and white

❖ Piece of scrap cardboard

❖ Old toothbrush

VARIATION

❖ Artist's acrylic paint in raw umber and white

❖ Scumble glaze

❖ Two lint-free rags

❖ Matte varnish

NOTE

Be sure you make up enough paint to cover all the walls in a room, not just the wall you are working on. Once you have mixed two colors, or diluted a color with water, it is difficult to get a perfect match if you want to mix up some more.

STARTING OUT – STEPS 1 TO 4

1 Pour some blue water-base paint into a large bowl or paint can and dilute it, using three parts paint to one part water. The water-base paint used here is only a few shades darker than the one already on the wall — sponging is most effective when it is subtle.

2 Put a large dollop of this diluted paint on a clean plate or small dish to use as your palette. This way, you can avoid dipping the sponge into the paint can and oversoaking it, which could create drips and splotches of paint on your wall.

3 Dampen the sponge in water, then charge it with the paint on the plate or small dish. Test the sponge on a piece of thick paper or cardboard to find the best "side" of the sponge before you start on the walls.

4 Start sponging in a corner first, then move out onto the main area of the wall. Vary your hand position and movement as you work, aiming for an even texture.

NATURAL SEA SPONGES

Natural sea sponges are not cheap, but they are certainly the best choice for sponging walls. The effect they produce is pleasing to the eye in its variety and lack of uniformity, an effect that is virtually impossible to capture with a man-made sponge. If you cannot afford a natural sponge, tear small pieces from an artificial sponge to achieve a natural look. Experiment on a piece of cardboard before you start on the walls, using different parts of the sponge, different angles, and varied hand pressures.

CREATING THE EFFECT – STEPS 5 TO 8

5 When you sponge the edges of the wall, for example near baseboards, fireplaces, or windowsills, use a piece of cardboard as a shield. Avoid oversponging and building up the color in these areas.

6 When you have completed one wall, take a step back and look at the wall from a distance. You may see some gaps or areas where the sponging is uneven. Tear off a small piece of the sponge and use this to add paint to these areas.

7 In a bowl or paint can, mix together some blue and white water-base paint to make a paler shade of your original color. Dilute it using three parts paint to one part water, as before.

8 Following the procedures in Steps 2 to 6, sponge this paler color onto the wall. Sponging on a paler color will brighten the whole paint effect.

SPONGING ON AND SPONGING OFF

"Sponging on" is one of the easiest and quickest of all the decorative painting techniques to master. Sponging on two different shades over a basic color gives a more interesting and opulent effect than simply using one color. Dab the sponge on delicately, changing its position and wringing it out frequently. "Sponging off" is done with a dry, clean sponge, which is used to lift a glaze from the wall surface. Work on a small area at a time, applying the glaze with a large brush and sponging off before it has a chance to dry.

VARIATION - MARBLED FIREPLACE

1 In a large bowl or paint can, mix together one part raw umber to six parts scumble glaze. Add a little water to make a thin, creamy "tinted transparent" glaze. This is the base glaze so make sure you mix up enough to cover the entire fireplace.

2 Prepare the other "veining" colors, each one on its own palette. Make up one of the colors using one part raw umber to two parts scumble glaze; mix up the other color with one part white acrylic with two parts scumble glaze.

3 If this is your first time marbling, you should only work on one section at a time. First, paint the base glaze onto the fireplace. Don't worry about a perfect finish—the glaze should cover the entire surface but can be thicker and thinner in places.

4 Scrunch up a lint-free rag and dab the crumpled side over the surface of the fireplace. Twist and turn the rag as you work without forgetting the corners. Rescrunch the rag from time to time to avoid a build-up of glaze on the rag.

THE COLORS OF MARBLE

Fantasy marbling can be carried out in any color combinations you want: black and gold, for example, is an exotic combination. If you are going for a more authentic look, however, you should study examples or photographs of the real thing. Two of the most frequently reproduced are Carrara marble, with a white base, pale gray clouding, and gray veins; and serpentine marble, which is green. The strong yellow of Sienna marble is broken by distinctive dark veining. Use a combination of effects if you feel adventurous.

CREATING THE EFFECT – STEPS 5 TO 8

5 Now, start to add the darker veining color. Using the No.3 sable brush, paint on veins by twisting the brush around, varying the pressure, and pushing the brush away from you. Remember that veining should be fragmented, uneven, and resemble cracks.

6 Continue adding veins of darker color, making sure you paint right into the corners and edges of the fireplace. Vary the tone of the veins by thinning the veining glaze with a little water. Be careful not to overload your brush and make sure you exhaust the paint on your brush before loading the brush again. When you have finished, wash the brush with water.

7 Now add veining with the white glaze, using a clean No.3 sable brush. Add white veins so that they follow the darker veins and cross over from time to time. Hold the brush far from the tip, as this will loosen your style.

8 When you have added all the veins, scrunch up a clean lint-free rag and lightly smudge the veins by twisting and rolling the crumpled rag over your work. Be careful not to overdo it—you don't want to remove the veins.

PROFESSIONAL TIP

If marbling is to look at all convincing it should be done on the smoothest surface possible. If necessary, sand the surface smooth before applying a base coat. When working with oil glazes, remember that they readily attract dust, so vacuum and dust the room you will be working in the day before you start. Make sure the room is free of drafts and that your brushes are also dust-free. Tiny fibers from wool sweaters or cardigans could also ruin your finish, so wear cotton or synthetics when painting.

FINISHING IT OFF – STEPS 9 TO 12

9 Dampen a clean sponge with water and dab and drag the sponge in places to remove some areas of glaze and reveal the background color. This will create depth to the paint effect, but resist the temptation to overdo it.

10 Dip an old toothbrush in the veining glazes and spatter spots of color here and there over your work. Don't do this all over the fireplace—a small spray will suffice.

11 Working quickly now, as the glaze is probably beginning to set, use a badgerhair brush to blend and soften all the painting. Use diagonal short strokes interspersed with wavy strokes.

12 When the glaze is completely dry, paint the fireplace with two coats of matte acrylic varnish, leaving enough time for the varnish to dry between coats.

OTHER EFFECTS

Decorative paint finishes are achieved for the most part by applying a semitransparent paint, or glaze, over a base coat, then distressing it so that the base coat shows through. The patterns created depend on the tools you use. For a stippled effect, use a stippling brush.

In rag rolling, which gives a crushed velvet look, the glaze is removed with a piece of lint-free cloth rolled into a sausage. Vary the effect by changing the tightness of the roll. A combed effect can be achieved by dragging a steel or rubber comb through the glaze.

CUTTING A MITER

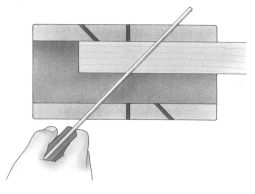

External left-hand miter

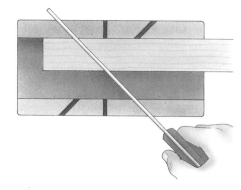

Internal left-hand miter

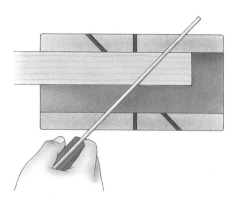

External right-hand miter

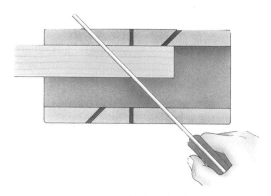

Internal right-hand miter

USING A MITER BOX

A miter box is used to cut any material that will fit between the two sides of the box, called the fence and the baseboard, and is used to make two ends fit neatly at a corner. When the miter box is used for cutting a cornice, place the "wall edge" against the larger side of the box furthest away from you (the fence) and the "ceiling edge" against the smaller side (the baseboard). Place a saw across the box and cut in the direction for an internal or external miter. See page 18 to find out what is an internal and external corner.

INDEX

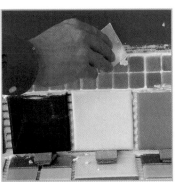

SIMPLE REMODELING: *Acknowledgments*

The author would like to thank and acknowledge the hard work of the following people:

Sally Walton for being my wife; **Dave Wellman** for his craftsmanship; and **Steve Differ** for always being there with a helping hand.

Marshall Editions would also like to thank **Philip Letsu** for design assistance; **Andrew Sydenham** for additional photography; and a special thanks to **Alma** and **Serena Schwartz**.